I0171618

ATHLETE'S MINDSET

Volume 4

Mental and Emotional Health Tools

Become A Leader

Team Unity * Courage * Leadership * Confidence * Visualization

Amy Twiggs

#1 Best Selling Author

ATHLETE'S MINDSET ACADEMY

Author's Note

Throughout this book I have used examples from many of my personal clients' lives. To ensure privacy and confidentiality, I have changed their names and some details of their experience. All of the personal examples from my own life are accurate and have not been altered.

To order additional materials or trainings associated with this content, please contact:

Flippinawesomecoaching@gmail.com, amy@athletesmindsetacademy.com, or www.athletesmindsetacademy.com.

First published 2021.

Paperback ISBN: 978-1-949015-22-5
E-book ISBN: 978-1-949015-21-8

Athlete's Mindset Academy
www.athletesmindsetacademy.com
Saint George, Utah 84790

ATHLETE'S MINDSET ACADEMY

For Emilee

I've been intrigued by your reactions to life and to others since you were small. In relationships, you have always been mature beyond your years. You don't need others to validate or motivate you. You just do good. You just are good. You spread positivity everywhere you go. Your ability to let others be who they want to be without judgment is fascinating. The impact you have had on my life by loving unconditionally inspires me to see where I can improve. Your superpower of limitless love and incredible acceptance is undeniably needed in our world.

Notice

This book contains discussions about mental and emotional health topics and problems. I have taken my experience, skills, training, education, research, and knowledge to formulate the systems and content provided in this book. I am not a physician, therapist, or scientist. If you should have any medical, emotional, or mental concerns regarding this material, please refer to your primary care physician, a medical consultant, or a professional therapist. In addition, please be advised that I cannot be held responsible for medical, mental, or emotional decisions you make as a result of reading this book. I waive all liability claims associated with the content in this book. This book is created for the sole purpose of opening your eyes to new possibilities, healing your heart, expanding your mind, and allowing the innate power you hold inside of you to grow exponentially as you dominate in and out of your sport.

Contents

ACKNOWLEDGEMENTS

Picking up another mindset and performance book about confidence and motivation in sports is proof of your commitment and your belief that there are answers to your athletic problems.

Considering the unending information available to athletes and coaches and the number of systems that just don't work, I commend your effort and willingness to give it another try. I want to encourage you to keep going until you achieve exactly what you have set out to do. Don't let my words or anyone else's determine how you will realize your goals. You must find your own path. You already have all the answers inside of you at this moment. In fact, if that is the only piece of information you take away from this book, it would have been worth reading. I believe in you. I believe you already know exactly what to do. You just didn't know that and didn't believe that yet. But, once you have finished this series, you will know. It's possible you will see things you haven't seen yet; you will know things you haven't known yet; and you will achieve things you have imagined yet.

To Tyler. I always wondered what it would feel like to receive a 10.0 in a big competition during my athletic years. I no longer wonder. A 10.0 life is what I get to enjoy daily with you. I love you.

To my four awesome kids who stop to give me hugs, bring me food, wrap me up in blankets, and recognize my passion for what I do and who I am. I hope you all run with your passions and open up to the endless possibilities available to each of you. You continually unveil your greatness to me and show me how to be more present, how to love unconditionally, and how to be better at playing every day.

To my clients, who allow me the opportunity to show you your minds when you would rather shut that door, when you would rather hold on to fear instead of letting yourself go toward fearlessness, and when you choose to believe in new possibilities instead of looking to your past for evidence of your

1

capabilities. Your breakthroughs fuel me to keep going. You allow me to be there working through what you think and feel during your athletic successes and failures. Your courage to feel terrible and open up to emotional pain fills me with great desire to learn and serve you better every day. Each of you has made my coaching experience and life more meaningful. Keep being Flippin' Awesome! You totally got this!

My Passion

"You must not have learned anything in your psychology classes at Stanford to dare suggest that coaches and parents don't cause pressure in their athletes. Obviously, you are not a sports coach or a parent, otherwise you wouldn't have said such a thing." This was a coach's comment on a post I sent out regarding the need to teach athletes about pressure and emotional management tools.

For the past twenty years, I have taught hundreds of athletes how to visualize success, affirm their way to confidence, and use cue words to stay focused during big competitions. I was once passionate about getting more athletes to "see" in detail what they wanted to experience on the field and in the arena, but now I "see" I was wrong. I wasn't wrong in teaching visualization and affirmation, goal setting and obtaining dream ideas for athletes, but rather, my methods for achieving those things were based on outcomes instead of the process. I believed if you could see something, you could achieve it. Now I know that just because I see success, I won't necessarily obtain success. There is much more to the equation for that result to take place.

And when I say equation, that is exactly what I mean. Success is much more formulaic than you might think. The way to win can be broken down to simple math. The way to consistency is math. The way to get more of what you want is, again, math.

What kind of math am I talking about? I teach athletes how to nail that beam routine, how to increase their free throw stats, how to shave time off their

100-meter backstroke race, or how to kick the field goals successfully every time. That is just one plus one equals two.

But what is even more exciting and fascinating for me to teach is how to make one plus one equal infinity. This is where I do not shy away from telling coaches that they can calm down and stop worrying about thinking they are the cause of pressure in their athletes.

Pressure is just one of ten thousand documented emotions. Emotions, in and of themselves, don't harm anyone.

The reason coaches believe they can personally cause pressure in an athlete is because they truly believe they have that kind of power. Unfortunately, this is because most coaches and athletes don't have the tools to understand that no one has that kind of power—no one has the ability to actually cause another person's emotions. Emotions are always within the individual's control and never come from outside. Emotional power has nothing to do with words or actions of something or someone else.

Once I teach athletes where pressure comes from and how to manage the amount of pressure they want to feel in any given situation, they feel empowered and in control.

Now, what coach or parent would not want their athlete to feel in control and powerful instead of powerless and afraid? When athletes understand these tools, they will no longer choose to believe that their parents or coaches can cause them to feel pressure.

I used to teach traditional sports psychology tools. I used to believe they were the key to athletic success. However, the more I learn, the more I train, the more knowledge I obtain, the more I realize that none of those tools matter if you don't understand the "why" of how they work. The sports psychology tools I used to teach have much more significance now that I better understand what's going on cognitively and how to generate the fuel you need for more expedited success.

Emotions are the key to success in sports. Emotions are the power behind every win! In this book, I guide you to understand your power. You become the hero, knowing how to generate more control, more power, and more success.

INTRODUCTION

"Worry about loving yourself instead of loving the idea of other people loving you."

—Unknown

"If you're frustrated with someone, you're actually trying to control them and it's not working. If you're resentful toward someone, you've been trying to control them and the frustration has turned bitter because the control attempts continue to not work."

—Nicole Wrage

This book is designed to be a continuation of the *Athlete's Mindset* series. The contents of all four volumes together create the overall Success Strategy for you as discussed in Volume 1, Chapter 1. Volume 1 discussed the idea that no success or failure causes your emotions. You are the only one who has the power to create your emotions. Volume 2 explains how you can generate the emotions you desire at any given moment. Volume 3 shows you how to dominate your game and execute your plan by using your power and emotions.

Each page in this book also has a specific purpose. They are to help you learn how to create more meaning and purpose in your sport by using all the tools in this series. Purpose is found in what you are choosing to do in this very moment. The greatest part of any sport is the relationship you create with yourself. Who are you at any given moment? Do you like the person you are becoming? Is this the best version of you? Are your choices leading you to where you truly want to go?

This volume will address tools that can help you create a deeper relationship with yourself as well as with your team and coaches. By using the methods provided in this book, you will become the team player your coaches recruited you to be and the athlete you want to be.

This past year, I coached a high school football team. The team had not yet won a game. I was invited to share some things with the group. The head coach later commented that he hadn't expected to have me back after the first team coaching session. However, the team won their first game of the season that weekend. He asked me to come back again and said, "As long as my team wins, you can come back." The team made it to the second round of the playoffs that year. It was exciting to see the coaches and athletes apply the tools each week and then come back to talk about what they learned, what worked, and what didn't.

The week before the first playoff game, we worked on visualization skills. The quarterback decided to practice the process of visualization each night as if he had already experienced the emotions at the end of the upcoming game and was just recounting the game over in his head before bed.

This particular team was not expected to win. In fact, at half time, they were down by two touchdowns. Much of the crowd started to leave before the second half. The head coach said he felt different going in to talk to the team at halftime. He reminded them of what they were capable of with a very calm and confident tone. The team went back out to surprise the fans by winning the game.

I was pulled aside after the next week's mental strength coaching session by an assistant coach who told me that after the quarterback of this team had thrown the winning pass, he ran up to this coach and said, "Coach, I lived it twice!" This young man had practiced believing, feeling, and seeing the results he wanted to create ahead of time, knowing he was capable of achieving those results. He had a déjà vu moment and was privileged to relive the experience in person during the actual game. He left the game with the same feeling he had generated night after night.

Preplanning your success and living it through visualization will create déjà vu experiences like this one throughout your sports career and life. Knowing these tools is nice. Applying the tools is powerful. "Living it twice" is a reality for many athletes; it can be for you too.

YOU GOT THIS!

CHAPTER 1

There May Not Be an "I" in Team, but There Is a "Me"

"Love yourself enough to set boundaries. Your time and energy are precious. You get to choose how you use it. You teach people how to treat you by deciding what you will and won't accept."

—*Anna Taylor*

In this chapter, you will learn how to build and manage your relationships with yourself and those around you. A relationship is a mental construct. The most important piece of any relationship is what you think about you. Your thoughts about you will change how you show up around others and your overall experience in any given relationship.

***

Emilee, my youngest daughter, loved being a competitive gymnast. She would beg to go to the gym an hour early and she often stayed after workouts to get extra help on her weaker skills. She woke up at 5:45 every morning to get some extra conditioning in before school. She was determined to get strong enough to compete well and move to higher levels.

Thanks to her commitment to herself to become better, her confidence in herself that she would stay committed, and all her extra work and effort, Emilee won her events at state level meets. Eventually, she went to regionals with the state team.

Gymnastics is a high-impact sport, which took a serious toll on her legs. By the time she made it to state competitions, both of her knees and ankles hurt constantly. Emilee refused to quit despite the pain she was in. After her state competition, I intervened and made her take a break to let her knees recover.

Emilee tried other sports with less impact during her gymnastics break. She didn't like any of the other sports she tried. None of them appealed to her the way gymnastics did.

A year later, Emilee returned to noncompetitive gymnastics.

Emilee had a relationship with herself and gymnastics that was strong enough that she refused to do any other sport. The only person Emilee knew she could disappoint was herself if she didn't follow through with her dreams. She knew herself well enough to know that her thoughts about gymnastics made her happy. And that was enough for her.

The dynamic and success of any team is based on two factors: the amount of confidence each athlete has in themselves and their willingness to open up to their own negative emotions.

Yes, you read that right. Each *individual* athlete's self-confidence affects the overall dynamics and success of the team. That means that your relationship with yourself is more important to the team than your relationship with anyone else on the team.

You are the deciding factor in team unity. How you think about yourself has a greater influence on your relationship with your team than anything else.

Life is about relationships, and the greatest relationship you will ever have is your relationship with yourself. The best way to become the best athlete you can be is to work on your relationship with yourself. The only person you have to change in a relationship to change the relationship is you. The only person you *can* change in a relationship to change the relationship is you.

What Is a Relationship?

What even *is* a relationship? You might say that a relationship is how someone knows someone else. You're partially right. Relationships are thought-based constructs of your mind. A relationship is how you think about another person.

There are three parts to any relationship:

1. Your thoughts about who you are in regard to that person

2. Your thoughts about the other person

3. Your thoughts about what the other person thinks about you

A relationship does not require anyone but you to be a part of it because you cannot inject thoughts and emotions into any other human.

You cannot control what others think about you. You *can* control what you think about you and what you think about others.

What you think about you will always show up in how you act in any relationship. If you are insecure, you look for reasons that other people think you're insecure. You then act insecure to validate your fear.

One great way to clearly see what is going on in a relationship is by putting the three parts of a relationship into STEAR and SPEAR models, as taught in Volume 3 of *Athlete's Mindset*. Start with a STEAR Model to find out why you are feeling any discord, then move to a SPEAR Model to decide who you want to be at any moment in the relationship.

To be assertive, think about what assertive people probably think, feel, and act like. Practice those assertive thoughts, feelings, and actions in your relationships. Find evidence that you are an assertive athlete in any situation by choosing what to practice believing about you.

Strengthening Your Relationships

It only takes one person to create a great relationship: You! That is great news! You are always in control of your relationships with your teammates, coaches, and anyone else in your life because the only person you ever need in order to strengthen a relationship is *you*.

See your relationship clearly by asking yourself the following six relationship questions. The first three questions help you identify what the issues in the relationship are. The second three questions help you find solutions to those issues in order to strengthen your relationship.

Three Questions to Figure Out What the Problems Are in Any Relationship

Make sure you specify one person or thing that you are struggling with before you answer the questions. Answer the following three questions by doing a thought transfer (see Volume 3 for a review). These are thoughts you should take time to really consider and notice when you are around this specific person.

1. What do you think about you in this specific relationship? (How do you feel about yourself in regard to this relationship? How do you show up around this person?)

2. What do you think about the other person in this specific relationship? (How do you feel about them? How do you behave around them? What are some thoughts that come up when you think about them?)

3. What do you think this person thinks about you?

Once you have completed the first three questions, spend some time working through the next three questions. As you answer the next three questions, you will find you might be resistant to the ideas that come.

Three Questions to Figure Out the Solution to a Problem in Any Relationship

You don't have to believe the answers to these next questions yet, but you will want to answer them as if you were living the highest possible version of you as an athlete and as a person. If this part is difficult for you, imagine how you would respond if you were talking about someone that you really love being around.

Answer the following questions to figure out how you can solve any disconnected relationship. Run some SPEAR models using curiosity, assertiveness, and compassion in the E line. See what happens to your R line or relationships without trying to change the other person.

1. What do you want to believe about yourself in regard to this relationship? (If you were acting like the best version of you in this relationship, what would that look like? If you were feeling like the most kind and confident version of you around this person how would that feel? If you believed you couldn't be more thrilled to be around this person, what kind of thoughts might you have?)

2. What do you want to believe about the other person? (If the other person were your best friend, what would you believe about them? If the other person completely surprised you and was exactly how you wished they were, what would that look like?)

3. What do you want the other person to believe about you? (If you were always showing up as the best athlete, teammate, friend, etc., what would someone who respected and loved you think about you?)

The Secret Back Door to Build Any Relationship

The last question, "What do you want the other person to believe about you?" allows you to go through the back door of someone's mind and puts you in the driver's seat to *decide* what you want their behaviors and words to mean about you.

You can love that teammate or coach or parent and there is nothing they can do about it. This question makes relationships into a game that keeps you empowered and intentional about who you want to be in a relationship.

If you want a great relationship without trying to change another person, spend some time contemplating what you want to believe that others think about you, then practice that belief.

For example, one athlete believed his coach was trying to sabotage his possible college scholarship by benching him during a game. We went through the six questions and spent a lot of time deciding what he wanted to believe the coach thought about him. Instead of believing that his coach didn't think he was worth the time or that he had no talent, this athlete chose to practice believing that it was possible the coach hadn't ever had an athlete with so much passion and drive.

The thoughts this athlete practiced were, "My coach isn't sure what to expect of me. I'm not like any of his other athletes because I'm willing to take risks as I am becoming a stronger and more skilled athlete. . . and that's okay. He doesn't have to believe in me because I believe in me. I have big goals and this coach is showing me how to believe in myself at a higher level. I'm grateful for this coach."

These are all optional and available thoughts that any athlete can have when they have a coach who seems to be showing less than total belief in their future goals.

Put effort into applying the answers to question number six by actively finding evidence that those thoughts could be true. As you do this, you will always receive a net positive result of tighter team unity and a stronger bond with coaches.

Remember that every thought is available and optional to you right now. You can always decide what you want other people to think about you, then just believe it. No one can tell you what to believe. What would happen if everyone in the world chose to think they are 100 percent amazing and believed that others thought the same thing? How would that change things for everyone on your team? How would that change your athletic experience?

Change your entire season by practicing the new beliefs you found using this exercise. By changing your entire season, you'll likely change the season for your team, too.

Drop Your Rule Book

In every sport, there is a rule book that clearly states what is and is not allowed. When it comes to relationships with teammates and coaches, you often, unconsciously, write a rule book for your relationships that you believe should be obvious.

Your rule book for your relationships is your list of unwritten, unspoken rules of things you think everyone around you should be doing to make you happy.

The problem with your rule book is that no one ever lives up to all of your rules.

If you could write down all of the rules that you have created for people and the world around you, you might find that *you* can't even keep up with your own rules! Yet you expect others to know and live those rules even though you haven't told them how to play by your rule book.

The cause of most divided teams is not understanding the unwritten rule book that each player has for the other members of the team. Once this idea is presented and athletes start to drop their rule books, teams become unified.

Instead of communicating your rules with others, you may have just assumed they should know the rules and then you become defensive and resentful when they don't follow the rules they don't know about. When others don't show up the way you think they should, you believe they don't care about you or your position on the team.

If you believe that telling someone to act or say things differently will make you feel happier, you need to refer back to Volume 2 of the *Athlete's Mindset* series, which describes where emotions come from. No one is responsible for your happiness and you are not responsible for theirs. Waiting for a teammate or coach to show up for your rules will always bring you disappointment.

Here are some typical "rules" athletes have for teammates and coaches:

- Teammates should always play at their best level.
- Teammates should know I am ready and open.
- Teammates should include me in conversations.
- Teammates should know my strengths.
- Teammates should be supportive.
- Coaches should let me play more.
- Coaches should give me more praise.
- Coaches should believe in me.
- Coaches should not yell at me.

Letting go of relationship rule books will allow you to open up to what a teammate is saying without becoming defensive. It will build better relationships and communication with coaches. You won't wait for something outside of you to change so you can feel good about you. You will be more assertive, take more initiative, and open up to more ideas that serve your game.

If you want someone to keep one of your rules, have that someone be you. Practice following through with your own goals, dreams, and expectations. Drop your expectations that others will follow your rules and see how that feels.

You will feel empowered when you don't try to live up to someone else's rule book and when you stop expecting other people to live up to yours. Let your teammates say and do what they want. You decide how you want to show up for practice, what you want to do with your time and resources, and who you want to become as an athlete.

Quit Blaming

Humans like to hold on to negative thoughts about others. They like to find evidence that others are terrible. Holding on to negative thoughts about other people is like hugging a saguaro cactus; it's better to let go of the negativity than to keep holding on.

It temporarily makes you feel good when you can tell a teammate about the terrible play another teammate made. Why? Because there is a little dopamine chemical released when you feel like you are a little better than that teammate. You get a little rush of false "enoughness," thinking you aren't the only one who makes mistakes. You get a little "pseudo joy" from believing you might have a chance to be the top person on your team and get the coach's attention someday too.

This arrogance is human nature, but it is never athletically satisfying. Comparing yourself with other teammates will always leave you feeling "less than" in the end. Be aware when you feel an urge to complain about a teammate or coach, when you want to blame a ref or an opponent for a result, or when you think anything outside of you is taking from you in any way. All those things may or may not be true, but believing life is happening to you will only make you feel disempowered. It will not change the thing or person that you are blaming.

Whenever you find yourself blaming anyone or anything outside of yourself for how you feel, you will feel lost. Blame causes you to disconnect with the only person who has the power to make you feel anything—yourself. Blame feels temporarily relieving but ultimately leaves you resentful and empty.

The Thoughts of Others

Behavioral research shows that humans spend the majority of their time worried about the one part of a relationship that is out of their control: the other person's thoughts about them.

Some people may not like you. That's okay. Not everyone has to like you. You aren't for everyone to enjoy, and you don't really want to be. "You can't make everyone happy," the saying goes. "You aren't a jar of Nutella."

What others think about you is really none of your business. Even if the other person wants their thoughts to be your business, those thoughts are theirs, not yours.

What another person says to you or about you does not come from your thoughts. By understanding that the other person's opinions about you aren't your own thoughts and opinions about you, you can allow yourself to be curious about why the other person thinks those things and desires to share them with you—but you don't have to let those thoughts and statements affect who you are and how you feel.

You never have to accept the other person's opinions as a gift you're required to take. Other's thoughts are not yours. Stop plastering on a fake smile and accepting the unwanted thoughts as your own. Stop pretending that you even *want* to accept them.

You are always welcome to visualize yourself kindly handing the unwanted thoughts back to their owner. After all, the other person's thoughts will never belong to you without your permission.

Generally, when others try to give you their thoughts for you to believe, they are unsure if *they* even believe those thoughts. Most people don't take the time to really consider what they truly think about their own default beliefs.

Most people vomit subconscious words as a socially acceptable, habitual way of acting on perceived scenarios.

I have found that the more you focus on what you want to accomplish and the more you let others do what they want to do, the division between those who do and don't like your choices gets more and more clear.

What I mean is this: the more successful you become, the more you should expect outside voices to tell you that you can't do that, you shouldn't do that, and you're not good enough to be that successful. There are usually more people that support you than don't, but they are usually the quiet majority.

As such, others' words are *always* facts in any STEAR or SPEAR model (see Volume 3); they are just part of the situation. But remember: *you* get to choose what to make any fact mean about you, that's where your power is.

How to Deal with Difficult Teammates and Coaches

What makes a teammate difficult? What makes a coach difficult? How do difficult people act? What if there is no such thing as a "difficult person"?

To be clear, I'm not talking about situations or people who are abusive or behaving inappropriately in other legal or ethical ways. These are situations that require actions other than just changing your thinking, sometimes including legal action. If you are in a situation like this, please seek outside help. However, there are plenty of other situations that you may face in which people just seem to be "difficult"; these are the situations I'm talking about.

Are there difficult teammates or coaches on your team? At some point in your life, there will be someone who doesn't agree with you. You may think they are just "wrong," which just "makes everything difficult."

If you cannot think of anyone who is difficult, then you may be the person that teammates and coaches say is difficult. This doesn't mean that you *are*; it just means you think differently than they do.

The word "difficult" is just a label people give to someone when they wish that person would think the same thoughts as they do. Just because your whole team would agree that you have a "difficult coach" doesn't mean your team is right.

18

There are only people. Any descriptions beyond that will either decrease or increase your own personal energy level. The change in energy is only a result of the labels you attach to your teammates and coaches.

What's it worth to you to use your own power for your personal athletic progress? What is it worth to you to level up your game instead of giving your energy away to negative thoughts about a teammate?

Here are seven truths about "difficult" people that will help you decide what you are going to do with the energy you have:

- There is no such thing as a difficult teammate or coach.

- Thinking another person is difficult will only downgrade your life, not theirs.

- What you focus on is where your energy goes. If you focus on wishing another person would change, you stop growing and reaching your own dreams.

- Changing teams or coaches won't remove all the people with different opinions than yours. There will always be another person that you wish would think a little more like you.

- Your best mentors typically come from those that challenge you to get out of your comfort zone.

- Every human is of 100 percent worth. There is no human that is of more or less importance than you.

- Substitute "difficult" with a different label. The label you choose will either increase or decrease your energy.

Three emotions you can choose that work well when working with "difficult" people are curiosity, compassion, and gratitude. An easy place to go mentally is imagining the "difficult" person either is experiencing irreparable pain or has a family member experiencing such pain. When I ask an athlete what they would think if they knew their teammate or coach was going through something really tough, the athlete always softens and drops the fear-based story about that teammate or coach. Being curious about what that person may be thinking and feeling that causes them to show up the way they do is an easy way to better understand and get along with a difficult person.

The best way to know what you think about yourself in general is to work on a relationship with a person that you find to be "difficult." These are the best teammates or coaches to use as vehicles to increase your relationship with and confidence in yourself. Anytime you attach a negative description to a person or thing, you project your own fear toward that person or thing.

Whenever you catch yourself thinking a teammate or coach is difficult, do the following:

- Stop. Take a breath.

- Find the thought that caused you to feel a disconnect from that teammate or coach (hint: it's usually something like "They should be or act different.")

- Flip that thought. Find an alternative thought that causes you to increase your own energy and moves you toward actions that are aligned with the best version of you.

- Find evidence for the new thought. You will have to actively find evidence that your initial thought could be wrong or at least not helping fuel your actions productively.

Be clear about how you want to think about yourself when working to improve a relationship. This is the first step to creating a sincere, authentic connection with anyone. The best way to support your team is by first learning how to support yourself. When all athletes know what to expect of themselves, team unity is easily achieved.

Chapter 1 Highlights

- Every relationship is a mental concept. It only takes one person to improve a relationship.

- There are three parts to any relationship: your thoughts about you; your thoughts about another person; their thoughts about you. You are in control of the first two parts. You are not in control of what the other person thinks about you.

- By asking yourself six questions, you can learn how to build team unity.

- There is no such thing as a "difficult" coach or teammate.

- All relationships start with what you think about yourself.

- Asking yourself questions from the best version of you will open up solutions for more connection and team unity.

- No one should do or say anything. You get to do and say what you want, and so do other people.

Chapter 1 Extra Mental Core Workouts

Remove the Team Unity Mental Block

Athletes generalize what "other people" think about them. In this exercise, I want you to find out who those "other people" are and take action based only on what you think. When you want to feel more empowered and confident around any teammate, coach, ref, fan, or friend, then work through the following questions:

- What do people think about you now?

- If you succeed at every goal you set, what would they think about you?

- If you went for every goal and failed, what would they think about you?

- How are those people right about you?

- How are those people wrong about you?

- Are you ready to let them be wrong about you? Why or why not?

- What will you commit to believe about you no matter what others will or won't think about you?

Flip It in Four

In this workout, take a sentence that seems to come to your mind easily when things aren't working out your way and then flip that sentence in four different ways. You can flip it however you want, just work on flipping it. Here are a few examples of how you can flip your thoughts. Sometimes, you might find that you feel better just after flipping the original thought one time. If you don't, then keep flipping the thought until you see some perspectives that will create the best outcome for you.

- **Example: This shouldn't be happening to me.**

    o Flip 1: This should be happening to me.

    o Flip 2: This is happening; now what?

    o Flip 3: I am making this thing happen.

    o Flip 4: I am willing to let this thing happen without resisting it.

- **Example: I don't ever want Coach to yell at me again.**

    o Flip 1: I don't ever want me to yell at me again.

    o Flip 2: I don't ever want me to yell at Coach again. (We may do this mentally without Coach hearing our mind dialogue.)

    o Flip 3: Coach doesn't yell at me; he yells his thoughts out loud, then I let my thoughts decide if he is yelling at me.

    o Flip 4: I am willing to let Coach yell his thoughts about him while I manage my own thoughts about me.

Own Your Game

It's much easier to blame someone or something outside of you for how you feel. Whenever you take responsibility for your emotions, actions, and results, then you are truly empowered. Own what you think, feel and do. Use the following prompts to take back your power in any relationship.

1. Name a person or situation that you believe is causing you emotional pain.

2. Describe, in detail, how they are are making you feel.

3. Write down why you believe they have power to create your emotions.

4. How does believing this story serve you right now?

5. Look at your answers to #3. Ask yourself if this story is true, if it serves you, and if you want to continue believing that story.

6. Consider separating the facts of your story from your beliefs about the facts. Can you see that the story you choose is the cause of your emotional pain and not the facts?

7. You could let go of your story about this person at any time, couldn't you? Why or why not?

Personal Notes

_____

_____

_____

_____

_____

_____

_____

_____

_____

_____

_____

_____

_____

_____

_____

_____

_____

_____

_____

_____

_____

_____

_____

_____

_____

_____

_____

Personal Notes

_____

_____

_____

_____

_____

_____

_____

_____

_____

_____

_____

_____

_____

_____

_____

_____

_____

_____

_____

_____

_____

_____

_____

_____

_____

_____

_____

Personal Notes

Personal Notes

_____

_____

_____

_____

_____

_____

_____

_____

_____

_____

_____

_____

_____

_____

_____

_____

_____

_____

_____

_____

_____

_____

_____

_____

_____

_____

_____

_____

_____

_____

_____

CHAPTER 2

ME, MYSELF, AND I

*"I have come to the frightening conclusion that I am
the decisive element. It is my personal approach that
creates the climate. It is my daily mood that makes
the weather. I possess tremendous power to make
life miserable or joyous. I can be a tool of torture or
an instrument of inspiration. I can humiliate, hurt, or
heal. In all situations, it is my response that decides
whether a crisis will be escalated or de-escalated,
and a child humanized or dehumanized."*

—Johann Wolfgang Von Goethe

*"Talk to yourself at least once in a day, otherwise
you may miss a meeting with an excellent person in
this world."*

—Swami Vivekananda

In this chapter you will learn why it's important to separate you from your
sport. When you feel that you are nothing without sports, you become disconnected from who you really are. Your higher self is not based on your
next win in athletics; it's based on your opinion of you. Learn to love yourself
by appreciating yourself and taking time to take care of you. You are not your
sport. You are so much more.

***

When athletes tell me how miserable participating in their sport makes them,
I ask why they continue to play it. They quickly respond with "I am nothing
without my sport."

If you are like many high-level athletes, you probably started sports at a very young age. You don't know what life is like without sports. Your identity and value may feel intertwined with your status as an athlete, which is why wins and team inclusion feel so important to you.

The idea of living your life without the sport as your identity is scary to you. The fear of failure and losing negatively impacts your self-concept. The irrational thought process leading you to believe you are nothing without your sport is rationalized by working toward the next win.

Relying on a sport to fulfill your emotional needs can lead to long-term issues. Giving yourself wholly to one thing leaves little when that thing is gone. You are left with little self-worth and don't know what or where to go without that thing when you give your entire identity to the thing. Putting all your self-esteem into one activity is like putting all your money into one stock: if the stock drops, your money is gone. If your ability to perform drops, your self-esteem is gone.

So how do you build up your identity outside of sports? You take care of yourself. You realize you have worth outside of your sport. You take time to do things you enjoy outside of sports.

You learn to love you and your life, not just your sport.

By learning to love you and love your life, with or without sports, you will show up as a more present player. Learn to be your best company. You don't "need" a win to make you feel enough. You most certainly don't "need" a sport to be whole.

You may say you don't have time to focus on yourself outside of sports. This is a tragedy. You spend so much time devoted to mastering one piece of your life, but you dismiss yourself along the way. Without taking time out of your busy schedule for you as a human—not an athlete—you may forget who you are. You are an amazing, thriving, and wonderful person with unlimited potential.

You are more than an athlete.

What Is Self-Care?

My son used to play football in high school. He was a great athlete, and his team went undefeated for years. Eventually, though, he decided to quit. Why did he do it? He knew that in his football position, he was regularly at risk for serious injury. This was a worthwhile risk as long as he loved the game, but he didn't really care much anymore. His team always won and he no longer felt challenged; the risk wasn't worth the reward. He chose to leave his sport even though he was amazing at it.

My son cared about himself enough to know when he needed to quit. He's an inspiring example of how to care for yourself, even if that means quitting your sport.

I questioned a university athletic director, Greg Waggoner, after a podcast interview recently regarding the consistent use of mental strength coaching in the world of sports. His response was that he believes that "less than one percent on average use mental training regularly as a part of their practice in sports. Mental health is pro-level sports development. When your self-identity is tied to your sport, then your fear of losing causes you to rationalize the irrational. Athletes need to develop other parts of their self-concept."

Your number one priority needs to be yourself. This isn't selfishness; this is self-care. Self-care is your ability to be aware of what your body and mind are saying to you. Self-care is preventive care at the highest level. It's realizing your innate desire to explore, understand, and enjoy everything life has to offer you without limitations.

Self-care includes what you choose to eat, how much you let yourself sleep, what other nonsports hobbies you do, and any other activity that helps you be your best. The key to self-care is choosing to enjoy activities for no one other than yourself.

One of the best ways to truly enjoy your athletic experience is to learn to schedule consistent time for some self-care. Your brain and body seek your attention. The most important person you can take care of is you.

The side effect of taking more time for you is that you have a lot more of you to give to your team. Focusing on you doesn't take away from you or others;

rather, it adds joy to your life, and you show up at a higher playing level for your team.

If a team really needs you to perform for them, they need you as healthy as you can possibly be. If you don't take care of yourself emotionally and mentally, you won't be as reliable. On the other hand, your team will notice, your coaches will notice, and you will notice when you've been taking good care of you.

Consider what you think about spending time alone.

If you were your only company, would you enjoy that company? Do you like yourself as a teammate? Do you think you are awesome? Do you talk to yourself like you are your own best friend? Do you adore yourself and tell yourself how great you are?

Your answer to each question should be an enthusiastic "Yes!" This may seem odd and boastful. It's not. It's called self-care.

When you are jotting down your plan for the week, be sure to put you at the top of that plan. Don't miss dates with yourself. Don't justify skimping on your personal time. Don't rationalize neglecting the one person who can help you get to your highest potential. You need you to be able to fulfill all your dreams.

You are amazing, you are enough, you are favored, and you are capable of doing anything you want. Give yourself the compliments you wish others would give you. Thank yourself for not giving up, giving in, or complaining after a long plateau in your sport. Give yourself a pat on the back for showing up day after day and working hard to master one small move. Celebrate you every day, because you're pretty amazing.

Self-Appreciation

To appreciate something is to become aware of its worth. To appreciate yourself, you must become aware of your own innate worth.

When you invest money into something, it appreciates, or grows in value. The difference between this type of appreciation and self-appreciation is that your value is already infinite.

Investing time in yourself seems like it would increase your value. Really, investing time in yourself unveils to you the innate greatness you already possess. Once you recognize your innate awesomeness, focusing on new thoughts becomes easier and you can more easily recognize your infinite value. Your worth is undeniable.

Appreciate yourself by consistently considering and writing down what you love about you. If you took time to do this exercise, what would you discover?

Don't move on until you can identify at least one thing you love about yourself.

Now don't move on until you can find another thing that you love about yourself.

Repeat the last sentence.

It's worth recognizing your worth to yourself. Self-appreciation is not about boasting or being arrogant. Self-appreciation is about loving yourself just like you love others. When you appreciate an inspiring person, you are noticing their greatness. Take time to notice your own greatness. You were given this greatness as an unearned gift for being born. You don't need to take credit for it, just appreciate it.

Self-Worth

Self-worth is your value as a human being. It's the worth you were born with. You gained this worth just by being born. You are 100 percent valuable because you are a human being who is living your life right now. There is literally nothing you can do that will change your worth.

Self-Worth
Innate

Self-Confidence
Based on your thoughts

Self-confidence and self-worth are not the same thing. No one is born with self-confidence, but everyone is born with self-worth. Self-worth is your worth as a human being. Self-confidence is based on your thoughts about you.

Self-worth has nothing to do with your opinion of yourself. Your self-worth is inherently set. You are 100 percent of worth. No win or loss, no achievement or failure, can change your self-worth. Your enoughness has nothing to do with your skill sets and your opinion of yourself. You just are enough, whole, of worth, and 100 percent valuable and amazing. Chapter 4 goes into what self-confidence is in more detail.

Setting Boundaries

A boundary is a simple request that you make of someone to change something and how you will respond if they don't. Boundaries are not emotional management replacements. Boundaries are about managing your thoughts, feelings, and actions about you.

To make a boundary, simply ask someone to stop doing the thing that you would like to have stopped. Then, tell that person what you will do if they do not comply with your request. This is not a threat; this is a request made from a place of self-care. Having a plan for if someone violates one of your boundaries allows you to live with integrity regarding who you want to be and gives you power to act intentionally.

Boundaries feel uncomfortable for you if you haven't protected yourself emotionally in the past. By keeping your word and following through on your requests, you will gain more trust for yourself, more respect from others, and more empowerment in your life.

Boundaries exist only for you to design the life you want, not to manage the actions of others. No one can touch your emotional boundary. You set boundaries out of love for yourself, not out of the obligation of another person to change.

Setting boundaries to manipulate another person will cause you to feel out of control. You cannot control another human. Hoping another human will change so you can feel better will disempower you.

Does a coach yelling at you mean you are being bullied?

Bullying is a hot topic among athletes these days. Bullying can be a subjective, gray area without knowing the exact situation. I am not going to tell you at what point you should reach out to a higher administrator or seek help regarding the behavior of another person. However, in regard to self-care, you will want to know how and when to create boundaries.

Many parents of athletes believe that the definition of bullying is when a coach gives a lot of corrections and little praise at a loud volume. Maybe it is. Maybe it isn't. Instead of listening to the tone used, listen to the words being said. When the tone of voice is separated from the words being said, what changes?

Be very aware of the distinction between what you think is "motivational talk" and "bullying."

Be clear and clean with your own thought management when you are discerning the level of mismanaged mental and emotional behavior. Ask yourself if it is truly bullying or if it is simply someone correcting you so you can become better. If you are truly being bullied, seek help. If you are simply being corrected, accept the correction and move on.

I want to encourage you to separate the facts from your thoughts about those facts in any situation. Run some STEAR to SPEAR models to check yourself and make sure you are coming from the highest version of you instead of a place of fear.

If one of your boundaries is that you do not want a coach to yell at you, you will need to be clear about why you want that, what that means, and what you will do if the coach does yell. Don't expect the coach to stop yelling. You are not trying to change the coach, you are setting boundaries to take care of yourself emotionally.

For example, if a coach yells at you, you can say, "If you continue to yell at me, I'm going to leave practice until you are able to speak to me more calmly." This not only allows you to keep your power, but allows the coach to also decide how they want to respond. All you have to do is follow through on your boundary if the coach begins to yell at you again.

Just be sure you are not setting a boundary from a place of wishing that the other person was different, and that you are not hoping to feel happier if they fulfill your ultimatum. Set boundaries from your higher brain, not as a reaction to a lower brain fear.

It takes a lot of courage to communicate and follow through with boundaries. It won't take very long before others will respect your ability to do what you say you will do no matter what. You will respect yourself more and feel an increase of confidence as well.

You Are Enough, You Are Lovable

Very few athletes like to talk about love. Love isn't measured on the scoreboard. Can love impact how you perform as an athlete? I believe it can and does every day you step foot in practice or a competition.

Love is the best emotion and one that everyone seeks for. If you have the choice between feeling love or feeling hate, you would prefer to feel love. Your relationship with yourself will be the clearest indicator of your relationship with your team and coaches. Do you feel loved? Do you feel empowered by loving thoughts about yourself?

Love is increased by setting boundaries, taking responsibility for your emotions, and spending time to take care of yourself.

There is nothing you can do to make others love you more. Your ability to be loved isn't about you. Your lovability is not based on another person's ability to love you. If a team or coach doesn't care for you, that doesn't have anything to do with you. It's about their ability to care about you. You can't control others' capacity to love you.

If a teammate or coach doesn't like or love you, that is not your issue. Your ability to love someone has to do with your capability to feel love. The more you can feel love, the more you will open up to loving thoughts about others.

When a teammate, coach, or opponent does something that triggers disappointing thoughts for you, your choice to love them anyway isn't for them. It's for you. Choosing love only makes you feel love.

What you feel is always within your power to decide. It's okay if you don't feel love toward someone that you've harbored ill thoughts about. Just remember that you are the only one that gets to feel the emotion you create.

When you hate a teammate, you are the one feeling hate, not the teammate. When you feel love toward a teammate, you are the one feeling love, not the teammate.

When you are struggling to find believable, loving thoughts about a teammate or coach, try answering these questions:

- How do you want to feel right now?

- Are you willing to try feeling this feeling way in your relationship with this person?

- Would you feel more or less energy in practice by choosing this thought about this person?

- What are you afraid of if you do choose to love this person right now?

The best skill you can develop if you want to take your game to a higher level is to learn how to choose the emotion of love rather than hate.

Only you can control your ability to love and feel loved. You are always lovable and enough. Love is always for you, and never for another person. You get the benefit. So choose love. It really is the healing ointment and personal power you need to be aligned with your highest athletic self.

Learning to believe in yourself will change your athletic process. Challenge your brain when it offers the idea that you are not enough. You are not your brain and you are not just an athlete. You are an amazing, thriving and wonderful person with unlimited potential.

Chapter 2 Highlights

- Your identity is not defined by your sports and can change whenever you want it to.

- Self-care is an important area for athletes to develop in order to find more sources of joy outside of sports.

- Self-worth is set at birth. Self-esteem changes based on your thoughts about yourself.

- Self-appreciation is discovered as you take time to notice your own value.

- Boundaries are necessary to create self-care.

- Love is an emotion more athletes could generate to help their performance level.

- Love is a gift you give yourself.

Chapter 2 Extra Core Mental Workouts

A Letter to Your Retired Athletic Self

- Write a letter from your imagined retired athletic self, who is exactly where you want to be in the future. Have him/her give you some pro coaching advice. What would your future self tell you to start doing or stop doing? What would she/he tell you to enjoy or avoid more? What might that future self suggest as steps to get to where your future self got? Close your eyes, sit with your future self, and have a good heart-to-heart conversation. Then write it about it in your journal.

- Schedule a date and time within the next year or two to reread this letter. Put the letter in a safe place with a reminder of the day, time, and location of your letter in your phone.

- A Letter to the Beginner Athletic You

- This is a great tool to help you reveal old negative beliefs. Let yourself open up to emotions that come as you complete this workout.

- Write a letter to the younger athletic you. Think about the younger you who couldn't get enough of your sport. Consider the reason you wanted to join a team years ago. Then fill out a letter written to "you" as a beginner athlete.

- An example letter format

    o Dear _____,

    o I wish. . .

    o I'm disappointed and angry because. . .

    o I'm sad and discouraged because. . .

    o I'm sorry that. . .

    o I see now. . .

    o I'm proud of you because. . .

    o I love you for. . .

    o Love, Me

Find More Joy

Complete the following questions as a check-in along your journey of achieving goals.

- List ten things that bring you joy.

- Could you add ten more things easily to that list?

- What is your top source of joy outside of sports?

- What would you like your top sources of joy to be?

- How can you generate more joy and happiness in this moment?

- How can you make your current sports goals more fun?

- Continue seeking a variety of sources of joy. Your list is not exhaustive.

1:1 Game

An important part of building a relationship with yourself is learning how to question each situation. In this exercise, I want you to:

- Write about a situation in your life.

- Then, list ten ways in which you could shift the perspective of this situation.

- Lastly, notice how your emotions shift with each new perspective. What's it like for you when you tweak the story just a little bit, or from another person's view? How does that change your experience?

Personal Notes

_____

_____

_____

_____

_____

_____

_____

_____

_____

_____

_____

_____

_____

_____

_____

_____

_____

_____

_____

_____

_____

_____

_____

_____

Personal Notes

_____

_____

_____

_____

_____

_____

_____

_____

_____

_____

_____

_____

_____

_____

_____

_____

_____

_____

_____

_____

_____

_____

_____

_____

_____

_____

_____

_____

Personal Notes

_____

_____

_____

_____

_____

_____

_____

_____

_____

_____

_____

_____

_____

_____

_____

_____

_____

_____

_____

_____

_____

_____

_____

_____

Personal Notes

POWERFUL DECISIONS + COURAGE = LEADER-SHIP

"A true leader has the confidence to stand alone, the courage to make tough decisions, and the compassion to listen to the needs of others."

—Douglas MacArthur

"When you doubt your power, you give power to your doubt."

—attributed to Honoré de Balzac

In this chapter, you will discover that your power lies in your ability to make decisions intentionally. It takes courage and commitment to decide what you want and what you are willing to do no matter what. Courage is an emotion that is one step in front of fear. Using these thoughts and emotional management tools to make intentional decisions, you will feel more courageous and more powerful. You will become a powerful leader through your ability to make powerful decisions, manage your time wisely, and honor your plans.

***

What is a leader? Someone who leads is the obvious answer. Consider this: a leader is someone who has the courage to make powerful decisions and follow through with them. Someone who others look up to because they know they can depend on their leadership.

Leaders know how to manage their time effectively and make decisions instead of wasting their time in indecision. The key to leadership is having the courage to manage your time, make powerful decisions, and follow through with what you have already decided.

Developing leadership skills will produce a lot of rewarding results. Use the tools outlined in the *Athlete's Mindset* as you set goals to efficiently achieve anything you want. You will show by example how to be a great leader as you accomplish your goals and achieve great things.

Make Powerful Decisions

What makes you feel powerful? What makes you feel powerless? An economic crisis, a number on the scoreboard, an unexpected team change, health problems, a position transfer, another chaotic situation?

I once took surfing lessons with my daughter and niece in Maui. Our instructor set us up for success by holding onto the back of our board, telling us when to prepare, and giving us a little push as a wave came to get us moving forward. Each time I popped up into the proper position, I noticed my daughter or niece swimming toward me as they went back out for another try. Because I didn't want to hit them, my eyes were focused on where they were in comparison to where I was heading.

My surfboard seemed to gravitate toward them every time. I ran right into their boards while they were ducking underwater for protection. As I headed toward them, I repeatedly offered sincere apologies for what was about to happen. I felt anxious, frustrated, and a bit hopeless.

The instructor coached me to keep my eyes up and focused on the palm trees that were on the shore, instead of looking at my daughter and niece as I tried to avoid hitting them. He said to "stop looking where you don't want to go." That was a good idea, but even when I looked up at the palm trees, I noticed my daughter and niece in my peripheral vision. I was trying to trick my brain into thinking they weren't a problem. I continued to find myself headed for more unintentional, but inevitable, incidents. After a few rounds of running straight into the girls, I opted for plan B—to jump off the board before another collision.

My mind kept repeating the surf instructor's advice, "Stop looking where you don't want to go." I tweaked that sentence to be "what do I want to do?" I wanted to keep my right foot in the spot where I was told to place it. I wanted to relax more in my stance when I was up on the board. I wanted to angle my shoulders to the side a bit more so I could feel more balanced on the board, and I wanted to get to the palm trees. Once I focused on what I wanted to have happen, my surfboard "magically" obeyed.

Instead of drifting to the obstacles in my way (my daughter and niece) I focused on where my foot was going to go. Once I focused on my stance and mastered that piece, I focused on my shoulder angle, and then my focus immediately went to finding the two palm trees. I was getting more stable on the board, and I found myself looking for details in the palm trees. The palm trees became my grounding space, or the landmark for my eyes. With practice, each time I felt the instructor give me a push, I felt my body pop into position and my eyes enjoyed the view of the palm trees.

I had thought my daughter and niece were always in my way, but in reality I was in their way. I became the obstacle for them while I was working so hard to keep them from being an obstacle for me.

The truth is, other surfers were never the problem. The surfers around me were innocent by-swimmers.

As I began learning how to surf that day, I used my power to decide that my daughter and niece were going to be obstacles to my success. Did I know that was true? No, but that didn't matter. Using my power to focus on my predetermined decision led me to act like they were in my way before I even got up on my board.

Trying to avoid what you don't want to have happen attracts more of what you don't want to have happen. That was a powerless decision on my part. My daughter and niece chose to use their power, based on their knowledge of surfing, to decide the palm trees were their goal. That decision led them to surf to the shore and have continued long rides without any incidents.

It was never about the other surfers. I chose my own experience solely based on my thoughts about the two girls. The two girls did the same thing. Their experience was different, but the fact that there were other surfers all around us in the water was the same for all of us.

These types of situations can make you feel powerful or powerless. There is one myth worth debunking in order for you to be able to make powerful decisions. It is believing that any person or thing can cause you to feel anything.

The truth is none of those situations or surfers can cause you to feel any emotion. You have no one and no thing to blame for how you feel. Without this clear understanding, you might miss the most empowering gift you own. It exists outside the external situation. That gift is your own ability to make decisions.

Powerful decisions create powerful results. Decisions don't have to yield expected results to be powerful.

Every moment of your day is composed of your decisions. The power of agency motivates every habit. Your choice in this moment is your reward in some future moment.

You might believe that other people, other people's words and actions, past events, finances, positions, pandemics, injuries, or any other situation can *cause* you to feel something. This makes you feel like a powerless victim in your own life.

Life happens, and when it doesn't happen the way you hoped, you feel disempowered and defeated. If you live your life trying to extract power and pleasure from external situations, you will be left feeling disempowered and dissatisfied.

Everyone can agree that we are all living. Life is not good or bad, right or wrong. It's just life. If you believe you have a hard life or a terrible life, then you probably feel miserable. When you feel miserable, what do you want to do or not want to do? Miserable people spend time telling others about their miserable lives. What does this give them? More misery.

The missing piece to the puzzle regarding your own personal power in life is learning to own your ability to choose which thoughts to focus on. Your personal power is 100 percent in your control and comes from your thoughts. Choosing to believe you are always in control of your decisions causes you to feel powerful.

This little distinction between your thoughts and your situations seems so innocently simple. Learning to apply the concept to your life is difficult.

By distancing your thoughts from your situations, you obtain personal power. You recognize your ability to employ your gift of agency.

Living your life without intentionally using your agency is like owning the newest cell phone and leaving it unopened in its package. The phone has so much wasted potential sitting in its box.

Once you believe the fact that your thoughts are *causing* all of your problems and emotions, then you have been given the universe. Understanding this, you now know how to solve every one of your problems. The same thing causing the problems provides the solutions: your mind.

Powerful results require powerful decision-making skills, which lead to powerful action. Powerful athletes perform amazing feats. Powerful people influence millions of people to take action. The decisions you make will either increase or decrease your power.

Powerful people don't need to justify, cover up, excuse, or hide from their decisions. If you desire to do good and have developed the capability of making powerful decisions, then you will take full responsibility for every decision you make. You are willing to apologize when necessary, consider new opinions when you see a new perspective, open up to change, and seek knowledge in order to make more powerful choices. Your intentions will fuel curiosity, courage, and compassion that lead you to create more, connect better, and contribute at a higher level.

Powerless people destroy, disconnect, and take away. If you choose to not decide who you are, what you want to be, what you want to do, and why you want to do those things, then you are using your innate gift and power to hide in fear, behind blame and resentment. There is no upside to this. Trying to extract power and confidence from your life will leave you powerless. Choosing to generate power and confidence in your life will leave you powerful and peaceful.

What kind of power do you want? Do you want to create or destroy? Powerful decisions from a desire to create and do good will elevate, inspire, and energize, generating more power and resulting in purpose, connection, and contribution. Conversely, powerful decisions made to destroy will exhaust and dissatisfy you and leave you feeling burned out, desperate, and fearful. What are you spending your energy on and why?

Powerful decision making is a skill. Just like any new skill, making powerful decisions takes practice. Practice the following five powerful decision-making tools:

1. Foundation of Power

You may think your situations cause your feelings. This is incorrect. Your thoughts about your situations cause your feelings.

Exercise:

1. On a sheet of paper, draw three columns.

2. Label the columns: Situations on the left, My Power in the middle, Feelings on the right.

3. Situations Column: List all the "situations" in your life.

4. Feelings Column: Write how each situation makes you feel.

5. My Power Column: For every situation, ask yourself why you choose to feel that emotion, then put your answers in the middle column. Every thought is available and optional for you. Why are you choosing those thoughts? Claim your power. Intentionally decide what you want to believe about the situation.

6. Choose one of your intentional decisions from this column. Practice it. That is how you develop the skill.

2. Flip a Coin

When I throw a tennis ball to my dog, he catches it every time. If I throw two or more tennis balls to my dog, he sits and lets the tennis balls hit him. He can't choose one over the other.

When you have two or more great options, you can get stuck in a rut of indecision and confusion, believing you might make a "wrong" choice or that the "best" choice will lead you to potential regret. Either of these ideas will lead you to the point of mental fatigue. What happens when you are mentally tired? You don't make a decision. This is called decision fatigue.

Decision fatigue is a result of lingering in between choices. When you aren't willing to open up to feeling a possible negative emotion as a result of a decision, you negatively impact your energy supply. The more you add to your pros and cons list, the less likely you are to make any decision at all. Conserve your energy by making a powerful decision.

Instead of asking which tennis ball is better, just assign heads or tails to your two decisions and flip a coin. Don't let the tennis balls hit you in the head. Catch one and run with it!

Exercise:

1. Get a coin.

2. Write what decision each side represents on a sheet of paper.

3. Flip the coin and commit to the decision represented by the side the coin lands on.

4. Take action from that choice.

3. Future Success

When making a decision, you sometimes hesitate because you want to know the outcome. The fear of the unknown, or xenophobia, keeps you from making powerful decisions.

Exercise:

1. Imagine you could visit your future. You knew the outcome for each possibility ended perfectly and beyond your expectation.

2. Knowing they are all perfect endings, ask yourself, "What would I choose?" This is like living back from your future right now. You already know the reward. You already know which path you want to choose.

3. Take no more than ten seconds to decide. The truth is you already knew which option you would have chosen before you asked yourself that question. You were just trying to validate your decision by comparing and contrasting other possibilities. This takes time away from making that incredible reality happen now.

4. Flip It

Life is 50/50. Pain and joy are partners on every road to success. Success is standing on a podium made of failures. Although fear is always along for the ride, you just want to keep fear on the tail end with courage in the driver's seat. Don't resist and avoid the negative part of every journey. Allow it to be there as you move forward with more powerful fuel. Whenever you feel your motivation drop, your energy lessen, your power weaken, try this tool.

Exercise:

1. Find the Fear: Ask yourself, "Why am I afraid to make a decision?" Believing you "have to," "should," "shouldn't," or "need to" is never true. You don't have to do anything. Anything you choose to do is always because you are "willing to" or you "want to." Find your fear, then move on to the next step. Here are four common fears that lead to powerless decisions:

   a. Fear of not being enough

   b. Fear of missing out

   c. Fear of not getting that "thing"

   d. Fear of being rejected

2. Flip It: Take the main fear-based thought and flip it. It's possible that the opposite could be true. Whether or not you believe this thought isn't the point.

3. Find Evidence: List 5–10 reasons why it's possible that the opposite thought could be true.

4. Fine Tune: Your powerful decision-making skills will increase as you continue to find any fear-based lies that are disempowering you. Use your power to flip the thought, find evidence for the new thought, and act on that increased energy one tiny decision at a time.

5. Final Answer

By doing this exercise, you will know whether you are committed to your goal. Oftentimes you think that you are making a "powerful" decision, but you are not truly committed to taking action. If you knew you had to give someone ten thousand dollars if you didn't achieve your goal, what decisions would you be making today that you weren't making yesterday? What would you change? This strategy clarifies why you want a certain goal and how committed you are to achieving it. This is powerful decision making at its finest.

Exercise:

1. Think about a goal you want to make and why.

2. Write that goal down.

3. Find someone you greatly respect. Talk to them about your goal and decision to follow through with it.

4. Write their name down.

5. Tell that person, "If I choose to quit on my goal before (predetermined date and time), I will give you ten thousand dollars."

Make powerful decisions by being aware of what you are thinking and choosing your next thought wisely. Your innate gift of agency is the greatest asset you have. No one else has the power to use your agency for you. What you believe about getting to that next level is simply a choice. The choice is yours. The powerful decision is your responsibility. Your power comes in your ability to decide who you want to be in any situation. What do you think is possible for you? What will you decide today?[1]

---

[1] This section is similar to my chapter "On Making Powerful Decisions" in the book *Leadership in Trying Times,* edited by Arnold Sanow and Amy Twiggs (Speakers Without Borders, July 2020).

Pre-decide and Do It Anyway

Accomplishing any goal requires you to make powerful decisions ahead of time, calendar those decisions, then honor your calendar. The more you set up your decisions ahead of time, the more likely you are to take the next step toward your goal.

Setting and completing a goal as a leader is very simple:

1. Predecide what you want to do and why. Be very detailed.

2. Predecide all the things you think you will need to do, learn, develop, and believe to get that goal.

3. Predecide the priority of those things from #2.

4. Predecide the date you will complete the top one priority.

5. Predecide everything you will need to do to complete that one thing.

6. Predecide the priority of those things from #5.

7. Predecide when each thing will be done and write it on your calendar.

8. Honor your calendar.

You won't want to honor your calendar. Honor it anyway. You won't want to finish a project completely. Finish it anyway. You will think none of it matters. Take action anyway. You won't think you are getting any closer to your end goal by doing the one little preplanned action on your calendar. Do it anyway.

Time Management

Strong leaders know how to manage their time. Your time is the most valuable asset you have as an athlete. You can't make more time. What you *can* do is use the thought management tools to do more within the time you have. Time, like relationships, is a mental construct.

Time management is another way of saying thought or emotional management. What you think about time is what you will get from time. The way you spend your time is a reflection of your beliefs. What do you think about time right now? What do you think is wasting your time? What do you think is costing you your time? What do you want to create with your time in sports? What do you believe is a valuable use of your time?

The way you think about time reveals how much time you will have. As time is such an important asset, you will want to powerfully decide, preplan, and follow through with what you are going to do with it and how you want to think about time.

Time itself doesn't change, but your beliefs about time will change your use of it. Use the same tools presented throughout this series to help you intentionally decide what you want to believe about your time and how those beliefs impact your results.

Nine Quick Tools to Create More Time

We know every person has twenty-four hours in a day. The way you think about those twenty-four hours will either positively or negatively impact how productive your day is. Look at the following time management concepts and pick one to practice.

1. Having Abundant Beliefs: Practice believing you have plenty of time to succeed.

2. Preplanning: Put your plan on your calendar.

3. Making Powerful Decisions: You already know your answer to any choice. Don't spend time debating if you like what you've already decided. Move forward with courage.

4. Honoring Your Plan: Show up for yourself every time as if you are the MIP of your team because you are.

5. Taking Massive Action: Don't stop taking action until you get what you want. You have never "tried everything."

6. Constraining: Learn to let go of what is not necessary and focus only on what is.

7. Failing: Failure is also called learning and data collection. It is the only pathway to success.

8. Saying "No": Recognize the distractions that don't serve you or your goals; then avoid them.

9. Creating B- Work: Perfectionism is a dream stealer and a lie. Waiting for the perfect moment, angle, sunlight, muscle size, and level will result in more waiting. If you want to have more time and be a more impactful athlete to your team, then learn to enjoy creating excellent B- work.

The Emotional Key to Leadership

Courage is a key to becoming a great leader. Courage drives actions that most athletes aren't willing to take, such as following through with difficult conditioning assignments when the coach isn't watching. Leaders know how to generate the emotion of courage and always keep courage a step in front of fear.

Leaders have the courage to reach for the impossible goals. That courage drives them to achieve those goals, knowing they risk failure in the process. If each member on an athletic team used courage to set their goals and create their results, there would be no regret or blame at the end of a practice, game, or season.

When you see courage in someone else, it inspires you to get up and do something more with the time you have left, to help someone else feel the energy to rise and strengthen their resolve in something personally satisfying and serve the world in the end.

To be an amazing leader, you have to know how to produce courage. Courage is produced the same way any emotion is: by your thoughts. Volume 2 of *Athlete's Mindset* went into detail about how to produce emotions. If you've forgotten, go back to Volume 2 and review how to produce emotions.

Consider the following courageous thoughts:

- I was made for this.

- Impossible is temporary.

- If you can see it, you can create it.

- Everything I need is inside of me and ready to be seen.

- Everything is figureoutable.

- I'm possible.

- My capability is limitless.

- Everything is working perfectly for me right now at this moment. I just need to look for the evidence that is around me.

- The worst that can happen is a feeling. . . and I can handle that.

- Just watch me.

Let courage drive every goal you set. Observe how much faster you achieve the impossible for yourself when you use courage as your fuel.

Become a powerful leader by generating the emotion of courage. That courage will help you stay committed to your decisions, stick to your plan, and inspire others. Unite your team by being a courageous leader that makes the tough decisions.

Powerful decisions are actions caused by the emotion of courage being activated without wasting time with indecision. Preplanning your decisions and following through with them requires courage. Become a strong leader by making powerful decisions and managing your time wisely. Make powerful decisions by managing your emotions. Manage your time wisely by managing your thoughts about the time you have.

Chapter 3 Highlights

- Leadership is a skill you develop as you apply the tools from this series.

- Powerful decisions are made by using your agency at the highest level.

- Time management is a mental and emotional management tool.

- Productivity happens when you practice following through with your decisions.

- You are more productive when you follow through with your decisions.

- Goals are easy to write down; achieving goals requires you to do what you say you are going to do.

- Having the courage to stay committed to yourself and your goals will help you become a powerful leader.

Chapter 3 Extra Mental Core Workouts

Tip to Make Powerful Decisions at Practice

Ask yourself:

- When will I know if I have enough information to make an informed decision?

- How long will I give myself to make the decision once I do have enough information? (Decision fatigue is real.)

Make the decision. Move on. Period.

What Do You Believe about Your Time?

What you think about will happen. Based on your thoughts about sports and the time you have left to participate in sports, answer the following questions:

- What do you believe about time?

- What do you believe about your past time in sports?

- What do you believe about your current time in sports?

- What do you believe about your future time in sports?

- Do you believe you have enough time? Why or why not?

- What takes up most of your time in and out of sports? Why?

Look at your answers and see if you notice how your current results in your sport are proof of what you believe about your time and your sport.

What Are You Really Doing?

When you say you are overwhelmed, busy, or just can't do another thing, take a few moments to do the following exercise:

- List EVERYTHING you spent your time doing in the past twenty-four hours.

- Write down what your thoughts are about that list.

- Are these decisions getting you closer to your goal?

- Are there any changes you need to make to get you closer to your goal in a more productive manner?

- What if tomorrow was your last day participating in your sport? What would you do? How would you work out?

- Are you really spending your time aligned with the goals you set?

Elite Level Productivity

As an athlete, you understand the importance of using your time wisely. Here is a simple time management method to increase your production capabilities:

- Designate an hour to pre-plan your week.

- Make a list of every project and the tasks associated to each projects that you want to get done this week.

- Break down each task into smaller tasks.

- Allocate the expected time to complete each small task.

- Prioritize your list.

- Put each task on your calendar.

- Throw away your list.

- Honor your calendar.

Personal Notes

_____

_____

_____

_____

_____

_____

_____

_____

_____

_____

_____

_____

_____

_____

_____

_____

_____

_____

_____

_____

_____

_____

Personal Notes

Personal Notes

_____

_____

_____

_____

_____

_____

_____

_____

_____

_____

_____

_____

_____

_____

_____

_____

_____

_____

_____

_____

_____

_____

_____

Personal Notes

_____

_____

_____

_____

_____

_____

_____

_____

_____

_____

_____

_____

_____

_____

_____

_____

_____

_____

_____

_____

_____

_____

_____

_____

_____

_____

_____

CHAPTER 4

UNSTOPPABLE CONFIDENCE

"Confidence is a habit that can be developed by acting as if you already had the confidence you desire to have."

—Brian Tracy

"That which we persist in doing becomes easier to do; not that the nature of the thing has changed, but that our power to do is increased."

—Ralph Waldo Emerson

In this chapter, we are going to dive into confidence. Confidence is an ongoing topic among athletes, parents, and coaches. What is it? How can you get more? Why do you not feel confident in some situations but totally fine in others? Do you even need confidence to win games? Is there a difference between confidence, self-confidence, and arrogance? This chapter will answer these questions. You will learn what confidence is and what it is not. You will learn how to obtain limitless self-confidence if you are committed to getting it.

***

"Who wants to go hiking tomorrow morning at 5:00?" my brother-in-law, Greg, asked the family during our trip last summer. I agreed immediately. The rolling mountains, wildlife, rivers, and overall open space made the area we were staying in perfect for a beautiful early morning hike.

Greg was outfitted and ready to go at 5:00 as promised. He chose quite a hard hike for us to do. We parked the car at the base of a steep hill and followed Greg up a rocky trail in the dark of the morning.

We made it to the pinnacle of that hill in good time and enjoyed the sunrise. As we were heading back down, I noticed movement to my right. I froze. Upon stopping, I noticed more movement through the brush to my left and then again just a couple feet ahead on the trail.

I saw a small dark snake first, then a little red-yellow-black snake, and lastly, a snake that looked a lot like a baby rattlesnake. Growing up in Arizona had made the last one easy to identify. My mind raced with the rhyme about red and black a friend of Jack or yellow on red and something about a fellow. I couldn't figure out how to tell what kind of danger I was in, but my lower brain was blaring fire alarm signals that this was dangerous and needed immediate attention.

I was completely frozen and could neither speak nor move as I watched the snakes begin to move slowly around me. I considered my exposed ankles as snake candy.

I called for Greg, but I don't think my whisper was very effective. Greg was too far ahead to hear my whispered calls for help. He eventually stopped to see why my husband and I weren't following him.

When he saw what I was looking at, he stopped to consider the situation. Greg's chosen course of action was to laugh, scoop the snake up onto his walking stick, and fling it at me.

Having a baby snake thrown at me had not crossed my mind as an option to get me out of my decision paralysis, but the flying snake was probably the only thing that got me to move. I had no idea what I could do to get out of the circumstance, but getting snakes thrown at me certainly wouldn't have been one of my choices!

I loudly vocalized my disagreement with Greg's "rescue." He continued to laugh and asked if he had forgotten to let me know that this was called "Snake Hill." Snake Hill got its name from the fact that when the sun comes out, the snakes come out. Greg handed me one of his walking sticks to help me feel safer the rest of the way down. I don't know what I would have done without that walking stick.

Why was Greg able to easily scoop up a snake while I stood frozen with fear? How was he so confident around snakes that he chose to use Snake Hill to train for hunting season?

In this story, Greg's confidence was a result of his knowledge about dealing with snakes. He felt confident he knew what to do if he encountered a snake. What does confidence mean to you?

What Is Confidence?

Confidence is your ability to trust yourself. It's how you show up for yourself and what you think about yourself. I use the term confidence in a general sense to mean self-confidence when I talk about emotions, but confidence can be an emotion or a result of courage, commitment, and skill development. The two types of confidence are confidence gained from learning a new skill and self-confidence from your thoughts about yourself.

There is a difference between skill type confidence and self-confidence. Most athletes say they want more confidence. They believe that if they had confidence then they would do that thing or take that risk and they might be able to accomplish great things. Lack of confidence to do that thing is what holds them back. This type of confidence is gained through skill development.

Self-confidence, on the other hand, has to do with what you think about yourself, your ability to honor integrity with yourself, and how you treat yourself. If confidence is a feeling about your skills, then self-confidence is a feeling about yourself. Both categories of confidence are emotion based and can help you reach your goals.

What does confidence mean to you? What is the difference between confidence and self-confidence? Do you know where your confidence comes from? Do you believe you are a confident athlete? Why do you want more confidence? What will that do for you in sports? How can you get more of it? Do you believe you will be more valuable if you have more confidence? Do you think more people will like you? Will you like yourself more if you have more confidence?

Questions like these will help you pause for a moment and reconsider the purpose behind your desire for more confidence. A good reason to desire more confidence is to become the best version of you. A purpose outside of yourself is never a good reason to want more confidence.

Why Don't You Feel Confident?

So why don't you feel confident? You haven't learned how yet. You haven't trained yourself to trust yourself yet. You haven't worked on the thoughts you need to raise your opinion of yourself. Maybe you haven't considered a different perspective.

Your thoughts create your emotions. When you focus on a thought repeatedly, you create a belief. Your beliefs are what drive your actions.

If believing you have to be perfect all the time inspires you to take risks and open up to fear and failure, then keep that belief. If not, try on the idea that there is more than one definition of perfection. Maybe perfection means simply trying your best and giving your best effort. When you don't take an opportunity because you're afraid to make a mistake, you make the biggest mistake by not even trying.

When you think you have nothing left to give and it's too hard to move forward, remember this: there is *always* something more in you. Expand your mind. Think, "What else is possible right now? This isn't all I've got. What if it is possible to think differently about this situation?" These thoughts are the ones that will increase your confidence.

Confidence doesn't just rain down on some people and not others. Confidence is a skill you can master just like any other part of sports. Confident beliefs are easy to learn and practice, but like any skill, confidence takes regular effort. Practice thoughts that induce confidence and take time to form those beliefs into habits. Confident beliefs create confident results.

Three Pillars of Self-Confidence

Think of these three self-confidence pillars like a three-legged stool. When one leg is weak, the chair is weak. If individual members of a team strengthen all three pillars of self-confidence, then that team will perform at their highest level. The teammates you want standing next to you are the ones that are confident in themselves. They don't rely on or blame anyone or anything. It's your job to be that type of teammate.

Self-confidence is your ability to stay in integrity with who you are and what you believe. What you think of yourself is the foundation of your self-confidence and will influence every decision you make in sports and in your life. It's your relationship with you that influences everything. Trusting yourself, opening up to all emotions, and having a decidedly high opinion of yourself are vital to a person's confidence. Let's examine these three pillars of confidence in more depth.

Pillar 1: Trust Yourself

Trusting yourself means doing what you say you're going to do. Your relationship with you increases when you keep your word. Trusting yourself also means standing up for what you believe is right. Integrity with yourself is one of the best suggestions I can offer for an understanding of self-confidence. Integrity means to be whole, undivided, and undaunted.

Your integrity with yourself is reflected in your interactions with others. You make commitments to yourself and others and honor them. You take care of your mind and body. You are responsible, even when you'd rather do what others are doing.

Doing what you say you will do, no matter what—especially when you don't want to—is the foundational pillar of self-confidence.

When someone says they'll do something for you, but they never get the thing done, you lose trust in them. The same goes for you. When you tell yourself you will do something and then don't do it, you have divided your own intention. You've lost trust with yourself.

Saying you will do something then "hoping" you do it is called doubt. Self-doubt is the opposite of self-confidence. Doubt, confusion, overwhelm, worry, and self-pity are subcategories of fear. These emotions are not found on the playing field of confident athletes.

When you tell your coach you are going for something, are you ending that statement with a question mark or an exclamation point? Are you walking back down that runway or onto the court saying, "I got this?" or "I got this!"?

If you don't know what to expect of yourself, how can you expect anyone else to know what to expect of you?

How do you build trust in yourself? Start small. Preplan little wins. Tell yourself you will do something that you are willing to do every time and begin there. Making a plan and following through builds self-confidence because you learn to trust yourself. Consistently honoring your word to yourself in small ways will make it easier to follow through on the bigger decisions.

Nobody is born with self-confidence. Confidence is earned one decision made and honored at a time. Do what you say you will do when you say you will do it, and you will feel your self-confidence increase immensely.

Pillar 2: Embrace All Emotions

I once invited a large group of high-level athletes to a training about fear and failure. The coaches and team were excited. The day before the training was scheduled, I got a call from one athlete's mom, who we'll call Jane. Jane was appalled and irate that I would even *think* about using "That Word," *especially* in front of athletes. It was, apparently, incredibly irresponsible for me to talk about "That Word" in front of athletes.

"What word?" I asked. I was confused. What was "That Word"? I couldn't avoid using a word if I didn't know what the word was.

"You know, the topic you chose for the training," she replied.

"Oh, you mean fear?"

It was as if I had shot her with a rubber band. As Jane angrily sucked in a breath, I realized how paralyzed she was just by hearing the word "fear." She proceeded to tell me that by just saying "That Word," I am inviting more of it into the lives of everyone who hears "That Word."

If I were to give you the option of all your favorite foods from a silver platter or your least favorite foods from a gold platter, which would you choose? Most people would choose the food on the silver. But, as athletes, you say you want to have the gold—not the silver—winnings.

If I were to change food items to your favorite and least favorite emotions, you would probably again choose the emotions on the silver platter. You would essentially settle for silver so as not to feel the pain of the gold. Interestingly enough, the way the human experience is set up is that in order to get the favorite emotion from the silver platter, you have to also take the opposite emotion from the gold platter—you have to experience the painful emotion anyway! So you might as well go for the gold platter and actually get the gold while you're at it.

You want to feel happy? Feel sadness first. You want to feel undefeated? You need defeat as a reference. You want to feel confident? Become friends with fear.

Now, which platter would you say the emotion of confidence would sit on?

I want you to consider that the emotion of confidence includes every emotion on both platters. You probably wanted to believe confidence was on the silver, or "good feeling," emotional platter, but confidence is increased the more you open up to your emotions—positive or negative.

Review the chapter about digesting and allowing emotions in Volume 2. Processing your emotions will help you accept all your emotions, which will create unstoppable confidence.

When you are willing to open up to any feeling, knowing that is the absolute worst outcome you will have to endure if you take a risk, you will gain confidence.

Knowing you'll have to feel negative emotions, how much confidence do you want?

People with unstoppable confidence *earned* that level of confidence by feeling terrible half of the time. If they didn't feel 50 percent terrible, then they are not athletes with unstoppable self-confidence.

To know the feeling of confidence, you must first know the feelings of doubt and fear. Fear is just an emotion. Emotions are harmless. The more you welcome fear, the less fearful you become. Embrace your fear. That seemingly immovable fear will yield to your unstoppable confidence.

Pillar 3: Have a High Opinion about You

Self-confidence is your ability to stay aligned with who you think you are and who you want to become. An easy way to see what that looks like is to get your notebook out again and write the story of who you want to be.

Who you think you are compared to who you want to believe you are may be very different stories. Neither story is right or wrong; they just produce different results in your confidence level.

Just because you think you are strong and powerful doesn't mean it's true or false; however, *believing* you're powerful will increase your confidence. The energy you create by believing you are strong and powerful will lead you to more confident actions and results.

Self-confidence goes up and down based on your opinion of yourself. When your opinion of you is low, you feel low. When your opinion of you is high, you feel lighter, stronger, and more confident.

So, to have more self-confidence, simply have a decidedly high opinion of yourself. The only person whose opinion about you matters is *you*. You're pretty great. You are your own biggest cheerleader! You're fabulous, and you deserve that crown because you are innately amazing!

You may not feel self-confident. That's okay. You haven't developed the skill of feeling confidence yet. Like any skill, confidence takes practice. If your natural setting is to search for self-doubt, rigorously practice seeking thoughts that include high opinions of yourself in order for you to feel more self-confidence.

Confidence is just an emotion. All emotions come from thoughts that you focus on. Thus, what you focus on when you think of yourself will decide if you are feeling confident or not. Therefore, choose to focus on more confident thoughts—thoughts that will help you become who you want to be—to increase your confidence. You are amazing and deserve limitless self-confidence!

Confidence versus Arrogance

Believing you are 100 percent valuable and being self-confident is *not* the same as being boastful and arrogant. Boasting and arrogance is about comparing yourself to others in an effort to make yourself seem better than another person. Self-confidence is believing in your own strengths and worth as facts.

Boasting and arrogance are about comparison. When you compare your strengths to someone else's weaknesses, you gain a false sense of confidence. Confidence does not have anything to do with anyone else. When you tell someone else of your skill sets in an effort to prove your worth, then you are being arrogant. Worth is set. You can't prove it to anyone, not even yourself.

Believing you're better than someone else in hopes of increasing your own confidence actually has the opposite effect. Instead of feeling better about yourself by comparing, you feel an underlying fear that someone else could show you up at any moment.

In an attempt to defeat this fear, you have to continually compare yourself to others and find outside reasons why you are enough. This will drain your energy because there is no way to ever prove your enoughness. That, again, is inherent in you. Going around telling others how you are better than they are will only leave you feeling like you are less on the inside in the long run.

What you say to someone to build yourself up is just a projection of the underlying fear you feel about yourself. You don't want others to see your weaknesses because you don't want to acknowledge them. You are afraid of being less than what you seem in any way, so you make sure everyone believes you are enough. The only reason you would act arrogant is because you are insecure and fearful.

So how can you tell if you're being arrogant versus being confident? Val Douroux, a good friend, comedian, and owner of Electric Comedy, suggests writing down facts about yourself, then picking one and putting it in the sentence, "Not to brag, but. . ." This is a great exercise to help you learn the difference between being arrogant and simply knowing that you are capable and accomplished in certain areas.

For example, if you wrote down "I pour water like a boss," your sentence would be "Not to brag, but I pour water like a boss." That's a fact, so in this case, it would reflect confidence. If you wrote down "I pour water better than other people do," your sentence would be "Not to brag, but I pour water better than other people do." That's arrogance. You're comparing yourself to someone else.

When you are filled with self-confidence, you have no need or desire to see yourself or others as less than or better than you are. Believing in your own strengths and worth as a human being is true self-confidence.

Confidence as a Result

The confidence discussed earlier is the *emotion* of confidence needed to do things that you haven't mastered in your past. Confidence as an emotion leads you to take risks and try new things. Your willingness to keep going when you don't know the end result is a confidence that needs to be generated from what you think about you.

The second type of confidence—confidence in your ability to do something—is a result, not an emotion. In a SPEAR model, confidence would go in the R line instead of the E line in this case. You *are* confident instead of just *feeling* confident. The *fact* is you're confident. Confidence as a result *always* leads to more confidence as an emotion.

Gaining new skill sets increases your capabilities and therefore your confidence level. The more you are willing to learn and experience, the more capable and the more confident in your abilities you become.

Think about something you are really, really good at. Maybe you make fantastic, to-die-for pancakes or you pour water in a cup like a boss. Maybe you never spill when you drink from your water bottle during practice. You are confident in your ability to do something well. This confidence comes from experience and actions.

It's like riding a bike. When you first get on a bike, you might fall. Your confidence level grows the more you practice and the less you fall. Once you can ride without falling, you say you are a confident bike rider. Being a confident bike rider may lead you to ride more often and you will keep that confidence with your new capability. You are good at riding a bike and believe you can do it again.

Make a list of all the little and big things you can do right now. Think of things you can do now that you weren't able to do a year ago or ten years ago. That list is a confidence list. You can use that list to continue adding to your confidence by noticing when you attain a small win. Noting your many small wins helps develop your awareness, leading to small confidence increases.

Obtaining confidence as a result of genuine effort is goal oriented. For a review of goal setting, refer to Volume 3 of *Athlete's Mindset*. To get confidence as a result, you'll need the five Cs:

- Compelling Reason: What do you want and why? If you don't know why, then your goal won't stick.

- Commitment: You must believe 100 percent that you are going to continue to reach for your goal, especially when your brain says it's too hard. Plan for moments of overwhelm and move forward anyway. Stay committed to seeing your goal to completion. You've got this!

- Courage: This emotion will come as you commit and recommit to yourself daily. It will require courage to take the massive action toward your goals. Massive action just means you don't stop until you get that result. Even if you have tried "everything," there is still something else you can try! When you find yourself believing you've tried everything, remember that you haven't, and have the courage to try something new.

- Capabilities: This is the skill set you learn from focusing on one goal at a time. You want to win the Olympics? Do it! You now have the education and tools to make that happen.

- Confidence: Lastly, the coveted confidence—the quality that most people want more of. Confidence requires effort. The more you learn to trust yourself, the more confidence you will achieve. Reach your goals to gain trust in yourself and increase your confidence.

Draw a line in the sand from this moment on. Whenever you check in on what you think about yourself and you find your thoughts less than positive, gently remind yourself that those are no longer a part of your belief system. They are not bad, but they no longer serve you or your purpose. Replace them with better beliefs.

As an athlete, you are amazing at practicing a drill over and over until that drill becomes second nature to you. Take that same approach with your undesirable thoughts: replace them with something better until it becomes second nature to think more positive thoughts.

This one practice will make a huge difference in how you show up to your sport every day.

The ability to know that you are not your thoughts and that the thoughts you believe will reaffirm themselves in your life the more you entertain them will help you begin to wiggle your way free from those that don't serve you well.

You want confidence? Start trusting yourself to get your own back. Learn to show up for you, especially when you don't want to. Be your own best friend. You are the pro of your life and future. When you can say, "I've got this!" instead of "I've got this?" you will feel your confidence rise. There is no cap on confidence.

Chapter 4 Highlights

- Confidence is trusting yourself at the highest level.

- Confidence increases as you learn to open up to all emotions.

- Self-confidence is your judgment about yourself.

- Confidence is not arrogance; you don't compare yourself to others when you're self-confident.

- Confidence as an emotion is not the same as confidence as a result.

- Use the Five Cs to quickly increase your confidence as a result.

Chapter 4 Extra Mental Core Workouts

Moving from Obligation to Thrill

Find the differences between the following statements. Consider how they make you feel:

- I *have* to go to practice today. (Feel: stuck, pressured, trapped)

- I *should* go to practice today. (Feel: obligated, required, guilty)

- I *choose* to go to practice today. (Feel: decided, motivated, willing)

- I *want* to go to practice today. (Feel: desire, inspired, excited)

- I *can't wait* to go practice today. (Feel: blissful, ecstatic, grateful)

Try changing sentences with your own thoughts. See how the slight change of a word creates a change of feeling.

What Is Your Opinion of Yourself?

Write down everything you think about yourself. Don't hold back.

Once you are done, I want you to find someone to talk to. Maybe choose someone you know. Upon greeting that person, include "I want you to know that I think you are _____." In your conversation, read the list that you just wrote about yourself to that person.

What are your thoughts about this exercise? Do you want to do it? Why or why not?

Look at your list. How do those words make you feel? If you wrote down anything that might tear someone down on your team, then it's time to stop tearing yourself down. Adjust, erase, rip up, or burn any of those ideas that don't strengthen you.

You would never tell your best friend that they are not smart enough, pretty enough, fast enough, or good enough. If you wouldn't tell your best friend those things, then you should never allow yourself to talk like that to you either.

Life Is Like a Video Game

Every obstacle you overcome in life is similar to a level you pass in a video game.

Follow these steps to achieve your next goal or win your mental video game:

1. Decide on a goal.

2. Draw a video game character on the left side of a sheet of paper. Write your name above the character.

3. Draw a prize on the opposite side of the sheet of paper. Write your goal above the prize.

4. Draw at least five challenges, or levels, you will have to overcome between the stick figure and your prize. For example: Bottomless Cliff, River of Snakes, Steep Mountain of Doom, or Wall of Fire.

5. Write an obstacle that you might actually expect to confront while working on your goal. For example: Master a position, increase your speed, learn to be more assertive, or get more sleep.

6. For every obstacle you expect, write two strategies you believe you could take to keep moving toward the prize. For example: Practice new beliefs, generate preplanned emotions, learn a new skill, strengthen a specific muscle, schedule a conversation with a coach, or set an alarm for reminders.

7. As you complete each challenge, give yourself a mental "high five."

8. Move on to the next level until you reach your prize.

Personal Notes

_____

_____

_____

_____

_____

_____

_____

_____

_____

_____

_____

_____

_____

_____

_____

_____

_____

_____

_____

_____

_____

_____

_____

_____

Personal Notes

Personal Notes

Personal Notes

_____

_____

_____

_____

_____

_____

_____

_____

_____

_____

_____

_____

_____

_____

_____

_____

_____

_____

_____

_____

_____

_____

_____

_____

_____

_____

CHAPTER 5

LIVE IT TWICE

"I lived it twice."
—Landon Frei

*"If you want a new outcome, you will have to break
the habit of being yourself, and reinvent a new self."*

—Joe Dispenza

In this chapter, you will learn the steps to effective visualization. Visualization is a mental practice used to create a result in the mind, based on what you want the result to be in real life. Learning to build a relationship with yourself in order to grow in confidence and team unity is always easier when you can see what you are trying to become. Use the skills of visualization to see the highest version of you in specific goals as well as in specific relationships which, in turn, will efficiently get you the result you want.

***

I clearly remember participating in the national gymnastics team qualifying meet in the Delta Center in Salt Lake City when I was younger. Specifically, I remember trying out a new mental technique to prepare for this important event: visualization.

Every night for six months before the competition, I visualized a professional athlete performing my routines perfectly, then I tried to see myself perform the same routines the same way. At first, I would visualize my body twisting like a helicopter propeller during my floor routine, and I'd see myself constantly crashing and falling off of the bars and beam.

I panicked when the falls I'd visualized started happening during my workouts. I quickly realized I had to learn to see myself doing the techniques correctly in as much detail as possible. I began visualizing exactly how I wanted my routines to go, how I would feel while I did them, and what score I would get.

With practice, I learned to visualize myself doing my routines perfectly. I wouldn't fall or crash, and I wouldn't twist out of control like a crashing helicopter. I saw myself twisting my body at the right moments and landing every skill perfectly. I visualized the feeling of my leotard rubbing against my shoulders when I was doing my bar routine, my hair hitting me in the face when I turned on the beam, and my feet aching after landing a flip in my floor routine.

I would visualize the part of my floor routine I was most concerned about more than any other routine or event: a double tuck. I imagined how my body responded when my feet hit the ground; my quadriceps and glutes would tighten when I landed; my arms would raise simultaneously when I stuck the landing; and my eyes would focus on the blue carpeted floor first, then up to the crowd ahead of me. Above all, I would visualize myself feeling no fear.

My routines gradually got easier and easier in my mind, and unsurprisingly, they became more consistent in the gym.

As my routines got easier to imagine, other details about the competition became easier to see too. I could visualize myself walking into the arena wearing my competition leotard with my hair in the required tight, high ponytail. I imagined it would be slightly hot in the area, and the combination of the heat and chalk would make my hands feel too dry. I visualized the filled stadium seats and imagined how the loud cheering would drown out the sound of the announcer's voice over the intercom. I visualized every little detail I could think of. It was exciting to visualize myself in the meet.

When the day of the qualifying meet came, everything happened as I had visualized. The Delta Center was similar to my imagination: loud and full of people, with a slight heat that caused the chalk to dry out my hands. I wore the leotard I had seen, and my hair was in the traditional tight ponytail. I completed all my routines leading up to my floor routine exactly as I had visualized.

When I performed my floor routine—my biggest worry—I felt no fear, just as I had planned. I landed the double tuck I had agonized over just as I had visualized: my quads and glutes tightened, my eyes focused on the floor then the crowd, and my arms flew up into position to create what I had visualized as the perfect double tuck.

At that moment, I found my mind wondering, "Am I in bed at home or am I at the Delta Center?" It was an out-of-body experience, but it was one I had lived in my mind many times before.

What Is Visualization?

Visualization is the process of making a mental image of yourself doing something—such as reaching a goal or performing a technique perfectly—in as much detail as possible. It is an incredibly powerful tool used to become a better athlete and teammate.

Visualization has been proven to be effective in sports, and yet it is one of the least-used tools there is. Coaches and athletes claim they know visualization is important, but when was the last time you actually sat down, closed your eyes, and saw yourself winning your next big competition? When was the last time you felt the emotion you preplanned to feel after that competition was over?

When I ask athletes why they are not doing regular visualization routines, they tell me it's boring.

If you knew that boredom was the price you have to pay to be a professional athlete, would you be willing to be bored? I would hope so! Boredom is one of the least threatening emotions you could feel! You can handle feeling bored. I promise, it's worth feeling bored to become a better athlete.

Visualization is one of the most powerful tools available for athletes. Visualization allows you to refine actions and feel emotions you believe you will feel before any physical realization of that action or emotion actually happens. You see yourself doing something a certain way and feeling a certain emotion in a certain place at a certain time before it happens in reality.

Visualization can also help you improve relationships. By visualizing how you want to show up around the person you want a relationship with, you subconsciously become who you see yourself being around that person. The person you're visualizing a relationship with can be your best version of yourself if you want it to be.

During visualization, your brain sends messages to your muscles that imitate the messages it would send if you were actually doing the thing you visualize. This helps you create "muscle memory" for the desired goal or outcome.

Subconsciously creating muscle memory is one of the greatest aspects of visualization! It trains your brain to know what your best you looks and feels like in a situation you choose. Your body physically creates the result you see in your mind; as such, when you complete the goal you visualized, you won't feel surprised because you would have felt that result many times through your visualization practices. You literally live what you visualized.

When working on visualization, you need to be patient with yourself. As an athlete, you're used to practicing. Visualization takes practice just like any other skill.

Preparation for Visualization

Preparing mentally for visualization work can speed the process of realizing your goals. As an athlete, you know it's important to warm up and stretch to get your body ready for the upcoming physical exertion required during practice. The same goes for visualization. Warming up by placating your lower brain leads to a more effective visualization.

Your lower brain is always looking out for life-threatening scenarios. It doesn't like to feel discomfort, and therefore, it avoids change as much as possible. When you visualize new goals, you ask your lower brain to consider change as a possibility. Your lower brain will resist. It does this to protect you and keep you alive. The way you know your lower brain doesn't agree with your new goals is by noticing thoughts that feel like justifiable escape routes from your goals.

When beginning a visualization session, start by providing a safe physical environment so your lower brain can relax without working overtime to be on high alert for possible threats. Then, get rid of distractions so that your lower brain can't easily lure you away from the task at hand. Doing these two simple preparatory steps will help you create unconscious neurological impulses throughout your body that create on the outside what you are seeing on the inside.

By taking the time to develop your mind to clearly see what you want to see in an environment that feels safe, you will be able to transition to more difficult changes during visualization more smoothly and see your desired results faster.

Three Perspectives of Visualization

There are three different perspectives you should try during your visualization time: external professional, external personal, and internal personal.

External Professional

The external professional perspective is where you visualize a professional athlete or person perfectly performing the activity you visualize, from an outsider's perspective. In this case, you are the audience watching the person.

External professional perspective is the first perspective you use in visualization. To visualize from the external professional perspective, you'll have to do some research and find someone you want to be like. Get to know how this person moves and performs their skills. Find footage of that professional doing the skills you are working to perfect. Imagine the emotions that the professional is experiencing while you watch the footage. Watch the video of that person performing that skill until you've memorized the video. Close your eyes and watch the professional perform that skill perfectly in your mind, just like you watched on the video.

External Personal

Once you can clearly see every detail of the professional performing your skill from the audience's perspective, replace the professional with yourself. This is how you move from the first perspective to the second perspective.

The second perspective used in your visualization practices is the external personal perspective. The external personal perspective is where you visualize *yourself* performing exactly as the professional did, but instead of watching the professional doing the skill perfectly, you watch *yourself* doing it perfectly. This perspective might take a little more practice than the first perspective, as you won't yet have a video of yourself perfectly doing the skill you're working on.

Practice watching yourself perform the skill with ease and perfection. If you are unable to see yourself doing the skill perfectly, replace yourself with the professional until you can visualize the professional doing the skill right. When you can visualize the professional doing the skill perfectly, practice visualizing yourself again. Do not allow yourself to visualize yourself doing less than perfect performances. What you visualize will affect what you do in reality.

Internal Personal

Get comfortable visualizing yourself performing perfectly from the audience, then move on to visualizing yourself from your perspective as you perform the skill.

The internal personal perspective is the third perspective you should practice using. This perspective is where you visualize the action from the perspective of the person doing the action perfectly. It is literally visualizing what's happening from the perspective of the person performing the action.

The third perspective requires you to visualize the most details and is therefore the most difficult perspective to practice. It is, however, the most powerful of the three perspectives. While the other two perspectives are those of an outsider watching someone else do the skill or event, the third perspective is from the insider looking out around them. When you can consistently close your eyes and visualize every sensation you could feel as you perform the skill perfectly—from the perspective of the insider looking out—your body will learn how to perform the skill perfectly in reality before you even start practicing it.

How to Do a Visualization

Before you begin any visualization practice, do the preparation steps outlined earlier. Make sure your lower brain is in agreement with you so that your visualization is effective.

To begin a visualization, pick an event you want to visualize. The event you visualize can be anything you want to obtain mental control over before you experience it in reality. Events include specific skills, performances in competitions or games, relationships you want to work on, etc.

Visualize this event from a place of predetermined emotions. What emotions do you want to feel during this event?

Visualize what you want to have happen as if you already experienced it and are just reliving the experience. Be as detailed as possible. Go back to practicing the external professional perspective if you cannot see yourself doing a perfect skill while using the external and internal personal perspectives.

Your mind is powerful and memorizes what you want to have happen. Whatever you allow yourself to see, hear, feel, think, and believe is what your body will respond to. Do not allow yourself to visualize anything other than perfection. Visualizing yourself failing will cause you to fail in reality; visualizing yourself performing perfectly will help you to succeed in reality.

Here are some questions to help you figure out the details you want to visualize:

- What environment are you in? (Are you indoors or outdoors?)

- What is the temperature of the air around you?

- What are you wearing? How do those clothes feel? (Are they comfortable, do they chafe, are they loose or tight, etc.?)

- How do you feel during this event?

- Are there other people? If so, what are they doing and where are they?

- What sounds can you hear?

- If you're working on a relationship, how does the other person act around you? How do you act around them?

- If you're working on a skill, how does your body react when you do that skill?

  - What muscles loosen or tighten?

  - What positions are you in? (Feet spread apart, arms up, head tilted, etc.)

  - How does your body feel physically when you complete that skill? (Tired, sore, numb, etc.)

As you implement the tool of visualization in this chapter, you can see your own personal athletic success clearly in your mind. Visualizing yourself as the best version of you is how you can most benefit your team. The individual athlete's ability to visualize what they are capable of will help the team reach its highest potential.

Walk yourself into any experience by visualizing it first. The visualization process takes time and must be used consistently to see any significant outcome. Visualization takes consistent effort, but the results you'll see make the effort worth it.

Two Visualization Drills

It's important to make sure your lower brain feels as safe and nonresistant as possible, so learn how to visualize nonthreatening items—inanimate objects—first. Two great drills to begin practicing visualization are the orange drill and the fishing line drill. Practice these visualization drills from all three perspectives. Once you are confident in visualizing inanimate objects from the three perspectives, move on to visualizing yourself reaching your goal.

The Orange Drill

The orange drill is a simple way to practice visualization. To do this drill, you'll need an orange (or some other fruit). Hold the orange (or other fruit) and memorize every detail about it. Use as many senses as possible without damaging the fruit in any way. That means you can't eat the fruit. You'll need it later.

Close your eyes and visualize the fruit. Use all your senses to construct the orange in your mind.

What does the orange look like? Is it a dark orange or a light orange? Does it have lots of bumps or thick skin? Is it easy to peel in one try, or does it require many little peels? Does it have seeds and lots of juice? Can you see the juice spray as you peel the orange?

Once you think you've recreated the orange in your mind, open your eyes and look at your orange. How close was your mental construct to the real orange?

The Fishing Line Drill

The fishing line is a well-known mental focus drill that reveals the power of the mind rather succinctly. Without consciously using any muscles, you can move an object by just focusing on and seeing what you want it to do.

All you need is a short length of fishing line and a fishing weight or some other kind of line and weight. Tie the weight at the bottom of the string. The weight should be hanging freely from the thread.

Sit on a chair and rest your forearm on your leg or over the edge of a table. Hold the string with the weight in your hand between your thumb and index finger. Don't move your arm, hand, or fingers at all throughout this drill. Keep your eyes on the fishing weight. Focus all of your concentration there. Concentrate on the weight moving from side to side until the weight begins to move without you consciously moving anything physically.

Once the weight is moving from side to side, you can change the direction of the weight so it is swinging back and forth just by changing the picture in your head!

Challenge yourself by having the weight move clockwise and counterclockwise. Then visualize the weight coming to a complete stop.

This experiment teaches you about the power of the mind-body connection. When you visualize, nerve impulses travel from your brain to your body without you consciously making them travel. Your focus stimulates impulses in the little nerves and muscles in your fingers, making what you visualized happening to the weight become a reality.

The more you want positive change to happen and the more you will focus on the end results you are reaching for, the faster those results will come. The clearer you can visualize what you want to happen, the faster the weight will respond to your mental commands, such as changing direction.

There are only two reasons why the fishing line drill would not work:

1. You subconsciously do not want the weight to move and that resistance is picked up by your lower brain.

2. You are distracted and unfocused. You have confused and unclear thoughts sending too many contradictory messages at once.

You learn a lot about your ability to focus and your belief in the power of your own brain if you recognize that you are experiencing these issues. Both reasons are great indicators that you have room to work on yourself.

The orange and the fishing line exercises are good tools for increasing concentration and singularity of thinking. Continue to practice these exercises to see where you are in your concentration and visualization abilities. You will increase how quickly you can visualize the orange and change the direction of the weight as you continue to work on your visualization skills. Move on to visualizing yourself doing something to reach your goal in as much detail as possible once you've gotten the hang of these two drills.

Last Thoughts

The tools presented in the *Athlete's Mindset* series are based in cognitive science, innovative, and unique. They work together to create a sustainable winning mindset. If you feel uncomfortable trying the tools taught in this series, I want to invite you to stick with them long enough to see what could happen for you. I guarantee if you apply the tools, they will change the way you feel about your sport, the way you show up to your sport, and the level of performance you can enjoy during your athletic journey. Nothing will change for you if you don't apply the tools. If you want help with these tools, I invite you to join us at Athlete's Mindset Academy, where we take these tools and apply them to your life and sports.

Learning to overcome obstacles, become a mind ninja, develop emotional management skills, create an effective vision, and develop deeper relationships are great to read about—but they're even better in practice. You are *always* in control of how you want to think, feel, and show up in any situation. You have the power to choose what life experience you want to have. You can see what's possible for you by using these tools. Nothing is impossible and everything is happening for you!

Chapter 5 Highlights

- Visualization is a powerful tool that helps your brain clarify what you want to see before it becomes a reality. When you visualize, your body responds unconsciously and on a neuromuscular level to create what you focus on in your mind.

- There are three different perspectives of visualization: professional external, personal external, and personal internal.

- All three visualization perspectives require vigilant practice.

- Regularly practicing visualization prepares you for opportunities to live what you already visualized.

Chapter 5 Extra Mental Core Workouts

Find an Avatar

1. Decide on a professional or high-level athlete that executes skills that you want to improve upon in your sport. Study and observe how this role model responds to situations and performs each movement of your desired skills.

2. Use this professional example in perspective number one of your visualization practices.

3. Try using all three perspectives of visualization after you have finished your tension-relaxation breathing technique before bed for two weeks.

4. Write in your journal any changes you have noticed in your own skill development from experimenting with this technique.

Mindset Rehearsal

Think about one change you want to make in your sport. Visualize yourself as if you've already made that change. Answer the following questions:

1. What is different about you?

2. How do you feel having mastered this new goal?

3. How do you handle your next problem differently?

4. How do you behave and practice differently?

5. What do you imagine you could keep practicing?

Personal Notes

_____

_____

_____

_____

_____

_____

_____

_____

_____

_____

_____

_____

_____

_____

_____

_____

_____

_____

_____

_____

_____

_____

_____

_____

_____

_____

Personal Notes

Personal Notes

Personal Notes

_____

_____

_____

_____

_____

_____

_____

_____

_____

_____

_____

_____

_____

_____

_____

_____

_____

_____

_____

_____

_____

_____

_____

_____

_____

_____

_____

SUCCESS STRATEGY REVIEW

At the end of each volume, you have seen a Success Strategy Worksheet, an opportunity to see where the tools of each book fit into your overall game plan for success. I encourage you to use this worksheet and create more detail on your foundation and home, inside and out. Use the worksheet as a guide to know what your next step is toward your mission objective.

This volume focused on building additional skills to enhance your athletic journey, such as relationship building, decision making, time management, confidence, visualization, and others. In the Success Strategy Worksheet, you can see how each bonus skill from this volume adds to your strong foundation of truth, appreciation of your support system, and the ability to stay in your lane. Practice the skills taught in this volume and see how much time you save and how much energy you create as you complete one Success Strategy and move on to your next impossible goal.

You may want to refer back to Volume 1, Chapter 1 of *Athlete's Mindset*, where we discussed the importance of having an overall mission objective. In order to achieve an objective, you need energy to move forward. If the thought of your mission objective doesn't instantly stir something inside of you, then you may want to go back and reconsider the compelling purpose of what you are doing. You need to truly believe in your reason for working hard, falling down, and getting up again and again during practice. If your mission objective doesn't ignite a fire within you, then change it now. Go back and reconsider why you are putting all this effort into your sport, your physical training, your life.

Where Volume 4 fits into your Success Strategy Worksheet:

Chapter 1: Relationships can go in your lane or the other distractions lane, depending on whether you are making a relationship goal or if you are using a relationship as an excuse to avoid your own growth. Your relationship with you goes in your lane.

Chapter 2: Self-care is part of your lane. It is important to take care of you as a part of every growth pit goal that you set.

Chapter 3: Leadership, decision making, and time management can be growth pit goals as new skill sets; alternatively, they can be part of a goal that you are working on in your lane.

Chapter 4: Confidence is an emotion and a result; therefore, you can put that as a growth pit goal or as part of a goal you are working on in your lane.

Chapter 5: Visualization is part of your lane. It is important to use visualization for every growth pit goal you set.

Volume 4 Success Strategy Review

<u>SUCCESS STRATEGY: DOING THE IMPOSSIBLE</u>

MISSION OBJECTIVE:_____

ATHLETE'S
MINDSET ACADEMY

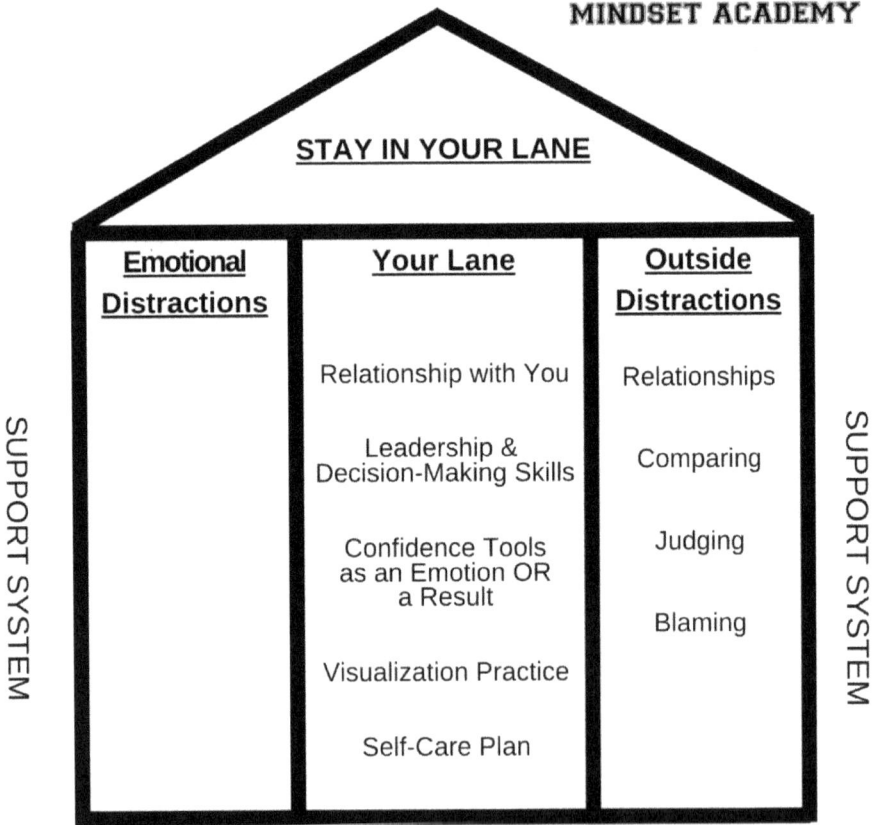

<u>STAY IN YOUR LANE</u>

<u>Emotional Distractions</u>	<u>Your Lane</u>	<u>Outside Distractions</u>
	Relationship with You	Relationships
	Leadership & Decision-Making Skills	Comparing
	Confidence Tools as an Emotion OR a Result	Judging
	Visualization Practice	Blaming
	Self-Care Plan	

SUPPORT SYSTEM (left side)

SUPPORT SYSTEM (right side)

FOUNDATION:
_____
_____
_____

Blank Success Strategy Worksheet

SUCCESS STRATEGY: DOING THE IMPOSSIBLE

MISSION OBJECTIVE:_____

ATHLETE'S
MINDSET ACADEMY

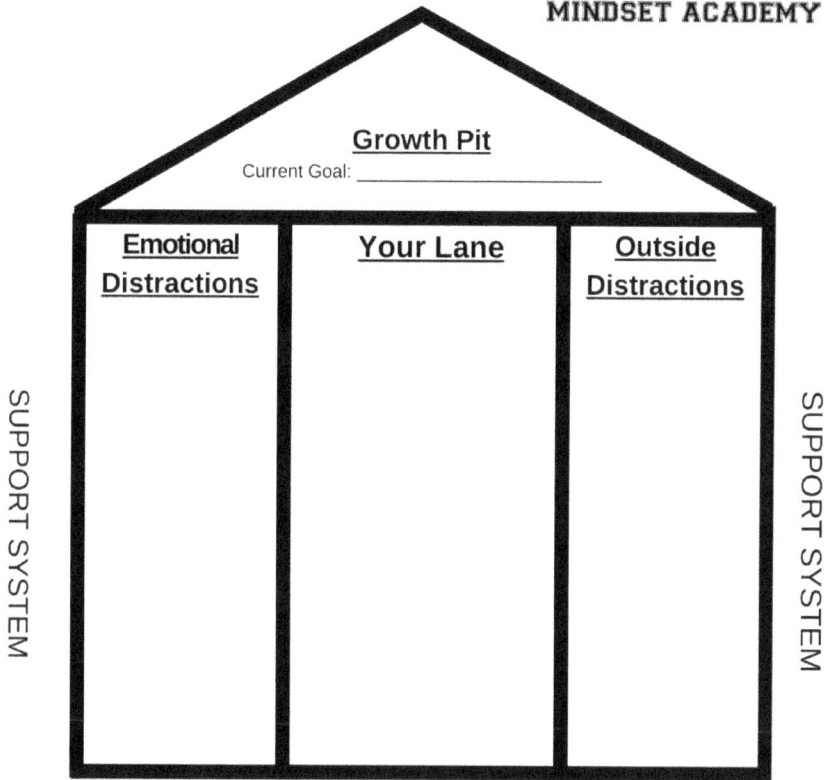

Growth Pit
Current Goal: _____

| Emotional Distractions | Your Lane | Outside Distractions |

SUPPORT SYSTEM

SUPPORT SYSTEM

FOUNDATION:

_____

_____

_____

ABOUT THE AUTHOR

Amy Twiggs, #1 Best Selling Author

Amy Twiggs is a wife and a mother of four incredible kids. She is a former elite gymnast and in 1993 she was a member of the National Women's Gymnastics Team. She received a full-ride athletic scholarship for gymnastics from Stanford University, where she obtained a bachelor's degree in psychology with a focus in health and development. She has worked in the behavioral health field for many years. She is the owner of Flippin' Awesome Coaching and co-owner of Athlete's Mindset Academy. She is professionally certified through The Life Coach School in mental and emotional health tools that greatly enhance clients' overall performance and life experience. Mental strength training and confidence coaching is her passion. Amy's education has provided many opportunities for her to give back to athletes and coaches. She currently lives in St. George, Utah.

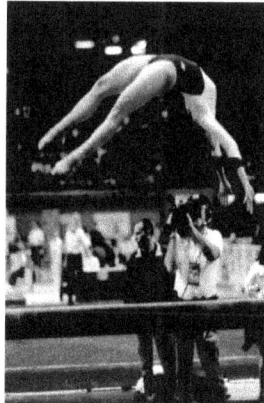

Contact Amy at:

flippinawesomecoaching@gmail.com

amy@athletesmindsetacademy.com

AthletesMindsetAcademy.com

www.ingramcontent.com/pod-product-compliance
Lightning Source LLC
Chambersburg PA
CBHW060333050426
42449CB00011B/2740